Property Of:

_____

The WOD Handbook

The WOD Handbook has been created as a reference for anyone wanting to learn more about the WOD's written and posted all over the world on white boards and websites everyday.

The WOD Handbook is designed for visual learners that want to see what all the major workouts looked like. We couldn't find a resource like this anywhere. So the idea to create an illustrated reference was born.

What is this Handbook? It is designed to be a visual aid to show what some of the most common moments are in each WOD.

What this Handbook isn't? It was never written to be a coaching manual. Nothing replaces the amazing coaches all over the globe helping to make people the best version of themselves they can be. If you are not sure about any WOD then your coach is the person you should consult.

We also hope that coaches will find this a useful tool to help them to educate their members.

CONVERSIONS:
To convert weights from lbs to kgs you need to divide lbs by 2.2. A handy conversion guide is in the back of this book.

Ladies weights are approx 30% less than mens weights if both weights are not listed on a WOD. If in doubt consult your coach.

MORE INFORMATION:
Further products are in development and will be available on:
www.wodhandbook.com

© 2014 by Peter Keeble
CrossFit® is a registered trademark of CrossFit, Inc.

Peter Keeble the author retains sole copyright to his contributions to this book. All care has been taken to maintain the accuracy of all workouts illustrated within this publication.

The Benchmark Girls

Angie

100 Pull-ups

100 Push-ups

100 Sit-ups

100 Squats

For Time
Complete all reps of each exercise
before moving to the next.

NOTES:

Barbara

20 Pull-ups

30 Push-ups

40 Sit-ups

50 Squats

5 rounds for time
Rest precisely three minutes between each round.

NOTES:

Chelsea

5 Pull-ups

10 Push-ups

15 Squats

Each min on the min for 30 minutes

NOTES:

Cindy

5 Pull-ups

10 Push-ups

15 Squats

As Many Rounds As Possible
in 20 minutes

NOTES:

Diane

Deadlift 225lbs

Handstand Push-ups

21-15-9 reps for time

NOTES:

Elizabeth

Clean 135lbs

Ring Dips

21-15-9 reps for time

NOTES:

Fran

Thruster 95lbs

Pull-ups

21-15-9 reps for time

NOTES:

Grace

Clean and Jerk 135lbs

30 reps for time

NOTES:

Helen

400 meter Run

21 Kettlebell Swing
1.5 pood (apx 55lbs)

12 Pull-ups

3 rounds for time

NOTES:

Isabel

Snatch 135 pounds

30 reps for time

NOTES:

Jackie

1000 meter Row

50 Thruster 45lbs

30 Pull-ups

For time

NOTES:

Karen

150 Wallball 20lbs 10'

For time

NOTES:

Linda
(aka "3 bars of death")

Deadlift 1 1/2 BodyWeight

Bench 1 Body Weight

Clean 3/4 Body Weight

10/9/8/7/6/5/4/3/2/1 rep rounds for time

NOTES:

Mary

5 Handstand Push-ups

10 1-Legged Squats (Pistol)

15 Pull-ups

As Many Rounds As Possible in 20 minutes

NOTES:

Nancy

400 meter run

15 Overhead Squat 95lbs

5 rounds for time

NOTES:

The New Girls

Amanda

Muscle-ups

Snatches (RX'ed M=135lbs, F=95lbs)

9 reps, then 7, then 5 of each exercise
For time

NOTES:

Annie

Double Unders

Sit-ups

50-40-30-20 and 10 rep rounds
for time

NOTES:

Eva

800 meter Run

30 Kettlebell Swing
2 pood (apx 72lbs)

30 Pull-ups

5 rounds for time

NOTES:

Kelly

1. 400 meter Run

2. 30 Box Jump 24" box

3. 30 Wallball 20lbs 10'

5 rounds for time

NOTES:

Lynne

Body Weight Bench Press

Pull-ups

5 rounds for max reps
There is NO time component to this WOD.

NOTES:

Nicole

400 meter run

Max rep Pull-ups

As Many Rounds As Possible in 20 minutes
Note number of pull-ups completed for each round

NOTES:

The Other Workouts

100 Pull-ups

100 Pull-ups

For time

NOTES:

3 Types of Pull-ups

**3 Weighted Pull-ups
45 pounds**

5 Strict Pull-ups

7 Kipping Pull-ups

10 rounds for time

r weighted pull-ups place a 45 pound dumbbell between the legs above crossed ankle nd jettison the dumbbell after third rep and continue with strict pull-ups and then the pping pull-ups. Coming off the bar or going to ground constitutes termination of a set

NOTES:

Annie Are You Ok?

500 meter Row Each Round

Dumbbell Thruster 35lbs

Sumo-Deadlift High-Pull

Burpees

MedBall Clean 20lbs

Wallball 20lbs 10'

21-15-9 reps for time

NOTES:

Bear Complex

7 Sets of the sequence:

Power Clean

Front Squat

Push Press

Back Squat

Push Press

RULES: No resting on the ground, even to re-grip, break up or combine movements in any way so as the following are met: the clean starts at the ground and finishes standing at full hip extension, the squats have to go below parallel and the presses finish locked out overhead. Jerking is acceptable as are squat cleans and Deadlifting then hang cleaning. The squats and the push press can be distinct or combined into thrusters .. but you can't receive the clean in a squat and go directly into a thruster .. stand first. There is not a time limit, rest anywhere anytime except on the ground!!! Starting weight: 65M/53F

5 round, rest between rounds as needed
Max load in the final round

NOTES:

Fight Gone Bad

Wallball 20lbs 10'

Sumo-Deadlift to High-Pull 75lbs (Reps)

Box Jump 24" (Reps)

Push Press 75lbs (reps)

Row (calories)

Every min move from through each of the 5 stations
The clock runs continuously
1 min rest between rounds before repeating. 3/5 rounds

NOTES:

Filthy Fifty

50 Box Jumps, 24"

50 Jumping Pull-ups

50 Kettlebell Swings
1 pood (apx 35lbs)

50 Steps Walking Lunges

50 Knees to Elbows

50 Push Press 45lb

50 Back Extensions

50 Wallball, 20lb 10'

50 Burpees

50 Double Unders

For time

NOTES:

GI Jane

100 Pull-up Burpees

For time

NOTES:

Nasty Girl

50 Squats

7 Muscle-ups

10 Hang Power Cleans 135lbs

3 rounds for time

NOTES:

Quarter Gone Bad

1. 15 secs of: Thrusters 135lbs
2. Rest 45 secs
3. 15 secs of: Weighted Pull-ups 50lbs
4. Rest 45 secs
5. 15 secs of: Burpees
6. Rest 45 secs

5 rounds for total reps

NOTES:

Tabata Something Else

Pull-ups

Push-ups

Sit-ups

Squats

32 consecutive Tabata intervals
(20 secs work, 10 secs rest)
Score total reps of all rounds

NOTES:

Tabata This

1. Squats
2. Row
3. Pull-ups
4. Sit-ups
5. Push-ups

20 secs of work followed by 10 secs of rest repeated 8 times.
1 min rotation break between exercises.
Each exercise is scored by the weakest number of reps (calories for the Ro

NOTES:

The 45's

45 Double Unders

45 Squat Clean 135lbs

45 Ring Dips

45 Double Unders

For time

NOTES:

The Chief

Max rounds in 3 minutes of:

3 Power Cleans 135lbs

6 Push-ups

9 Squat

Rest 1 minute
Repeat for a total of 5 cycles

NOTES:

CFT

CFT

Back Squat 1 rep

Shoulder Press 1 rep

Deadlift 1 rep

Warm-up with several sets prior to starting each exercise.
You get ONLY 3 attempts to hit your 1 rep max for each exercise
Your CFT score is the total of the highest weight completed in each exerc

NOTES:

The Hero Workouts A - Z

Abbate

1 mile Run

21 Clean and Jerk 155lbs

800 meter Run

21 Clean and Jerk 155lbs

1 mile Run

For time

U.S. Marine Corps Sergeant Matthew T. Abbate, 26, of Honolulu, HI, assigned to the 3rd Battalion, 5th Marine Regiment, 1st Marine Division, I Marine Expeditionary Force, based out of Camp Pendleton, CA, was killed on December 2, 2010, while conducting combat operations in Helmand province, Afghanistan.

NOTES:

Adam Brown

24 Deadlift 295lbs

24 Box Jumps, 24" Box

24 Wallballs

24 Bench Press 195lbs

24 Box Jumps, 24" Box

24 Wallballs

24 Clean 145lbs

2 rounds for time

Navy Chief Special Warfare Operator (SEAL) Adam Lee Brown, 36, of Hot Springs, Arkansas, was killed on March 17th, 2010 in Komar Province, Afghanistan, in a battle against heavily armed militants

NOTES:

Adrian

3 Forward Rolls

5 Wall Climbs

7 Toes to Bar

9 Box Jumps 30" box

7 rounds for time

U.S. Army Sergeant First Class Adrian Elizalde, 30, of North Bend, OR, assigned to the 2nd Battalion, 1s Special Forces Group (Airborne), based in Fort Lewis, WA, died on August 23, 2007, in Baghdad, Iraq, of wounds sustained from an improvised explosive device.

NOTES:

Alexander

31 Back Squats
135lbs/61kg

12 Power Cleans
185lbs/83kg

5 Rounds For Time

Staff Sgt. Alexander G. Povilaitis, 47, of Dawsonville, GA, assigned to the 570th Sapper Company, 14th Engineer Battalion, 555th Brigade, was killed in action on May 31, 2012 in Kandahar Province, Afghanistan, when enemy forces attacked his vehicle with an improvised explosive device.

NOTES:

Arnie

21 Turkish get-ups, Right arm

50 Kettlebell Swings

21 Overhead squats, Left arm

50 Kettlebell Swings

21 Overhead squats, Right arm

50 Kettlebell Swings

21 Turkish get-ups, Left arm

For time
With a single 2 pood kettlebell (apx 72lbs)

Los Angeles County Fire Fighter Specialist Arnaldo "Arnie" Quinones, 34, was killed in the line of duty on Sunday, August 30, 2009 during the Station Fire. His emergency response vehicle went over the side of the road and fell 800 feet into a steep canyon during fire suppression activities protecting Camp 16 outside the City of Palmdale, CA.

NOTES:

Badger

30 Squat Cleans
(M=95lbs. F=65lbs)

30 Pull-ups

800 meter Run

3 rounds for time

In honor of Navy Chief Petty Officer Mark Carter, 27, of Virginia Beach, VA
who was killed in Iraq 11 December 2007.

NOTES:

Barraza

200 meter Run

9 Deadlift 275lbs

6 Burpee Bar Muscle-ups

As Many Rounds As Possible
in 18 Minutes

U.S. Army Staff Sergeant Ricardo Barraza, 24, of Shafter, CA, assigned to the 2nd Battalion, 75th Range Regiment, based in Fort Lewis, WA, died on March 18, 2006, in Ar Ramadi Iraq, when he came under small arms fire by enemy forces during combat operations.

NOTES:

Bell

21 Deadlifts
185lbs/83kg

15 Pull-ups

9 Front Squats
185lbs/83kg

3 Rounds For Time

Air Force Senior Airman Bryan R. Bell, 23, of Erie, PA, assigned to 2nd Civil Engineer Squadron at Barksdale Air Force Base, LA, died January 5, 2012 at Camp Bastion in Afghanistan, of injuries suffered when his vehicle struck an improvised explosive device.

NOTES:

Big Sexy

1. 6 Deadlifts 315lbs/142kg

2. 6 Burpees

3. 5 Cleans 225lbs/102kg

4. 5 Chest to bar Pull-ups

5. 4 Thrusters 155lbs/70kg

6. 4 Muscle-ups

5 rounds for time

Sgt. Lance "Big Sexy" McLean, 38, of Biloxi, Mississippi, died on June 29, 2013, from a gunshot wound he sustained in the line of duty on June 28, 2013. Prior to his death, McLean served as a Sergeant with the Sheriff's Office, and as a member of the SWAT Team in Hood County, Texas.

NOTES:

Blake

150 ft Walking Lunge with 45lb plate held overhead

30 Box jump 24"

20 Wallballs

10 Handstand Push-ups

4 rounds for time

U.S. Navy Senior Chief Cryptologic Technician David Blake McLendon, 30, of Thomasville, GA, assigned to Naval Special Warfare Group 2 Support Activity in Norfolk, VA, was killed September 21, 2010, in a helicopter crash during combat operations in the Zabul province of Afghanistan.

NOTES:

Bowen

1. 800 meters Run

2. 7 Deadlifts 275lbs/124kg

3. 10 Burpee Pull-ups

4. 14 Single arm kettlebell thruster 7 reps each arm, 53lbs/24kg

5. 20 Box Jump 24" box

3 rounds for time

Captain Jeffrey Bowen, of Alexander, North Carolina, died July 28, 2011. The 37-year-old was a 13-year veteran of the Asheville Fire Department, assigned to Rescue 3. Bowen was fatally injured while fighting a four-alarm fire in a medical building.

NOTES:

Bradley

100 meter Sprint

10 Pull-ups

100 meter Sprint

10 Burpees

10 rounds for time
Rest 30 seconds between each round

U.S. Air Force Senior Airman Bradley R. Smith, 24, of Troy, IL, assigned to the 10th Air Support Operations Squadron, based in Fort Riley, KS, was killed on January 3, 2010, by an improvised explosive device in Zhari district, Kandahar Province, Afghanistan.

NOTES:

Bradshaw

3 Handstand Push-ups

6 Deadlift 225lbs

12 Pull-ups

24 Double unders

10 rounds for time

U.S. Army First Lieutenant Brian Bradshaw, 24, of Steilacoom, WA, died in Kheyl, Afghanistan, on June 25th, 2009, from wounds suffered when insurgents detonated a roadside bomb near his vehicle.

NOTES:

Brehm

**15 ft Rope Climb
10 ascents**

**20 Back Squat
225lbs**

30 Handstand Push-ups

Row 40 calories

For time

U.S. Army Sergeant Dale G. Brehm, 23, of Turlock, CA, assigned to the 2nd Battalion, 75th Ranger Regiment, based in Fort Lewis, WA, died on March 18, 2006, when he came under small arms fire from enemy forces during combat operations in Ar Ramadi, Iraq.

NOTES:

Brenton

Bear Crawl 100 feet

Standing Broad-jump 100 feet*
*Do three Burpees after every five broad-jumps

5 rounds for time
If you've got a twenty pound vest
or body armor, wear it.

Field Training Officer Timothy Quinn Brenton, 39, of the Seattle Police Department, was shot and killed in a drive-by shooting while on duty on October 31, 2009.

NOTES:

Brian

**15 ft Rope Climb
5 ascents**

25 Back Squat 185lbs

3 rounds for time

U.S. Navy Special Warfare Operator Chief Petty Officer (SEAL) Brian R. Bill, 31, of Stamford, CT, assigned to an East Coast-based Naval Special Warfare unit, died on August 6, 2011, of wounds suffered when his unit's helicopter crashed in Wardak province, Afghanistan.

NOTES:

Bull

200 Double Unders

50 Overhead Squat
(M=135lbs, F=95lbs)

50 Pull-ups

1 mile Run

2 rounds for time

U.S. Marine Corps Captain Brandon "Bull" Barrett, 27, of Marion, IN, assigned to the 1st Battalion, 6th Marine Regiment, 2nd Marine Division, II Marine Expeditionary Force, based out of Camp Lejeune, NC, was killed on May 5, 2010, while supporting combat operations in Helmand Province, Afghanistan.

NOTES:

Bulger

1. 150 meter Run

2. 7 Chest to Bar Pull-ups

3. 7 Front squat (M=135lbs, F=95lbs)

4. 7 Handstand Push-ups

10 rounds for time

Canadian Forces Corporal Nicholas Bulger died July 3, 2009 while on patrol in the Zhari cistrict of Afghanistan when an IED device exploded near his vehicle.

NOTES:

Cameron

50 Steps Walking Lunge

25 Chest to Bar Pull-ups

50 Box Jumps 24"

25 Triple Unders

50 Back Extensions

25 Ring Dips

50 Knees to Elbows

25 Wallballs "2-fer-1s"

50 Sit-ups

15 ft Rope Climb
5 ascents

For time

U.S. Coast Guard Lieutenant Junior Grade Thomas Cameron, 24, of Portland, OR, in training at the Aviation Training Center in Mobile, AL, died on February 28, 2012, when his unit's helicopter crashed into Mobile Bay in the Gulf of Mexico during a training mission.

NOTES:

Capoot

Push-ups

Run

Round 1: 100 Push-ups, 800 meters Run
Round 2: 75 Push-ups, 1200 meters Run
Round 3: 50 Push-ups, 1600 meters Run
Round 4: 25 Push-ups, 2000 meters Run

For time

Officer James Lowell Capoot, of the Vallejo Police Department, died Nov. 17, 2011, in the line of duty while chasing after an armed man suspected of robbing a bank. The 45-year-old, who lived in Vacaville, California, joined the Vallejo Police Department in 1993 and served as a motorcycle officer, motorcycle instructor, driving instructor and SWAT officer. He received two medals of courage, including one life-saving medal, as well as many other department commendations.

Carse

Squat Clean
(M=95lbs, F=65lbs)

Double unders

Deadlift 185lbs

Box jump 24"

21, 18, 15, 12, 9, 6, 3 reps per round for time
Begin each round with a 50 meter Bear crawl

U.S. Army Corporal Nathan B. Carse, 32, of Harrod, OH, assigned to the 2nd Engineer Battalion, 176th Engineer Brigade, based out of White Sands Missile Range, NM, died in Kandahar, Afghanistan, on February 8, 2011, from wounds suffered when insurgents attacked his unit using an improvised explosive device

NOTES:

Clovis

10 mile Run

150 Burpee Pull-ups

For time
Partition the Run and Burpee Pull-ups as needed

U.S. Army Second Lieutenant Clovis T. Ray, 34, of San Antonio, TX, assigned to the 2nd Battalion, 35th Infantry Regiment, 3rd Brigade Combat Team, 25th Infantry Division, based in Schofield Barracks, HI, was killed on March 15, 2012, in Kunar province, Afghanistan, when insurgents attacked his unit with an improvised explosive device.

NOTES:

Coe

10 Thruster (M=65lbs. F=45lbs)

10 Ring Push-ups

10 rounds for time

Army Sgt. Keith Adam Coe, 30, of Auburndale, Fla., assigned to the 1st Battalion, 37th Field Artillery Regiment, 3rd Stryker Brigade Combat Team, 2nd Infantry Division, Joint Base Lewis-McChord, Wash., died April 27th, 2010, in Khalis, Iraq, of wounds sustained when enemy forces attacked his unit with an explosive device.

NOTES:

Coffey

800 meter Run

50 Back Squat
(M=135lbs, F=95lbs)

50 Bench Press
(M=135lbs, F=95lbs)

800 meter Run

35 Back Squat
(M=135lbs, F=95lbs)

35 Bench Press
(M=135lbs, F=95lbs)

800 meter Run

20 Back Squat
(M=135lbs, F=95lbs)

20 Bench Press
(M=135lbs, F=95lbs)

800 meter Run

1 Muscle-up

For time

U.S. Marine Corporal Keaton G. Coffey, 22, of Boring, Oregon, assigned to the 1st Law Enforcement Battalion, 1st Marine Headquarters Group, 1st Marine Expeditionary Force, based in Camp Pendleton, California, was killed on May 24, 2012 while conducting combat operations in Helmand province, Afghanistan.

NOTES:

Collin

Carry 50lbs sandbag 400 meters

12 Push Press (M=115lbs. F=80lbs)

12 Box Jump 24"

12 Sumo-Deadlift High-Pu(ll) (M=95lbs, F=65lbs)

6 rounds for time

Navy Special Warfare Operator Chief Collin Trent Thomas, 33, of Morehead, KY, assigned to a Navy SEAL team based out of Little Creek, VA, was fatally shot on August 18, 2010, during combat operations in Eastern Afghanistan.

NOTES:

Crain

1. 34 Push-ups
2. 50 yards Sprint
3. 34 Deadlifts 135lbs/61kg
4. 50 yards Sprint
5. 34 Box Jumps 24" box
6. 50 yards Sprint
7. 34 Clean and Jerk 95lbs/43kg
8. 50 yards Sprint
9. 34 Burpees
10. 50 yards Sprint
11. 34 Wallballs 20lbs/9kg
12. 50 yards Sprint
13. 34 Pull-ups
14. 50 yards Sprint

2 rounds for time

Officer Michael "Freight" Crain, of Beaumont, California, died Feb. 7, 2013, when he was fatally injured by gunfire in an apparent ambush while on patrol. A former U.S. Marine Corps sergeant, the 34-year-old had been with the Riverside Police Department for 11 years, assigned to field operations and the SWAT Team.

NOTES:

Dae Han

800 meter Run with a 45 pound barbell

15 Ft Rope Climb 3 ascents

12 Thruster (M=135lbs, F=95lbs)

3 rounds for time

U.S. Army Sergeant First Class Dae Han Park, 36, of Watertown, CT, assigned to the 3rd Battalion, 1st Special Forces Group (Airborne), based out of Joint Base Lewis- McChord, WA, died on March 12, 2011 Wardak province, Afghanistan, from wounds suffered when enemy forces attacked his unit with an improvised explosive device.

NOTES:

Daniel

50 Pull-ups

400 meter Run

21 Thrusters
(M=95lbs. F=65lbs)

800 meter Run

21 Thrusters
(M=95lbs. F=65lbs)

400 meter Run

50 Pull-ups

For time

Dedicated to Army Sgt 1st Class Daniel Crabtree who was killed in Al Kut, Iraq on Thursday June 8th 2006

NOTES:

Danny

30 Box Jump 24"

20 Push Press
(M=115lbs. F=80lbs)

30 Pull-ups

As Many Rounds As Possible
in 20 minutes

Oakland SWAT Sergeant Daniel Sakai, age 35, was killed on March 21, 2009 in the line of duty along with fellow officers Sergeant Ervin Romans, Sergeant Mark Dunakin, and Officer John Hege.

NOTES:

DG

8 Toes to bar

8 Thrusters w/dumbbells
(M=35lbs, F=25lbs)

12 Walking Lunges w/dumbbells
(M=35lbs, F=25lbs)

As Many Rounds As Possible
in 10 minutes

U.S. Air Force Major Walter David Gray, 38, of Conyers, Georgia, assigned to the 13th Air Support Operations Squadron, based in Fort Carson, Colorado, died on August 8, 2012 from injuries suffered during a suicide bomb attack in Kunar province, Afghanistan.

NOTES:

Dobogai

8 Muscle-ups

**22 yard Farmer carry
50 lbs Dumbbells**

7 rounds for time

U.S. Army Captain Derek A. Dobogai, 26, of Fond Du Lac, Wisconsin, assigned to the 2nd Battalion, 35th Infantry Regiment, 3rd Infantry Brigade Combat Team, 25th Infantry Division, based in Schofield Barracks, Hawaii, died on August 22, 2007, in Multaka, Iraq, of injuries suffered when his unit's helicopter crashed.

NOTES:

Don

1. 66 Deadlifts (M=110lbs, F=75lbs)
2. 66 Box Jumps (M=24", F=18/20")
3. 66 Kettlebell Swings (M=1.5 pood, F=1.0 pood)
4. 66 Knees to Elbows
5. 66 Sit-ups
6. 66 Pull-ups
7. 66 Thrusters (M=55lbs, F=35/40lbs)
8. 66 Wallballs
9. 66 Burpees
10. 66 Double Unders

For time

U.S. Marine Corporal Donald M. Marler, 22, of St. Louis, MO, assigned to the 3rd Battalion, 1st Marine Regiment, 1st Marine Division, I Marine Expeditionary Force, based in Camp Pendleton, CA, died on June 6, 2010 while supporting combat operations in Helmand province, Afghanistan.

NOTES:

Donny

Deadlift 225lbs

Burpees

21-15-9-9-15-21 reps for time

Nichols, 21, of Shell Rock, IA, assigned to the 1st Battalion, 133rd Infantry Regiment, Iowa Army National Guard, based in Waterloo, IA, died April 13, 2011, in Laghman province, Afghanistan, of wounds suffered when insurgents attacked his unit using an improvised explosive device.

NOTES:

Dragon

1. 5 km Run

2. 4 minutes to find 4 rep max Deadlift

3. 5 km Run

4. 4 minutes to find 4 rep max Push jerk

For Time and Load

U.S. Army Captain Nicholas Rozanski, 36, of Dublin, OH Ohio National Guard, based in Walbridge, OH, died on April 4, 2012, of wounds sustained during an enemy attack by a suicide vehicle borne improvised explosive device in Faryab province, Afghanistan.

NOTES:

DT

12 Deadlift 155lbs

9 Hang Power Clean 155lb

6 Push Jerk 155lbs

5 rounds for time

In honor of USAF SSgt Timothy P. Davis, 28, who was killed on Feburary, 20 2009 supporting operations in OEF when his vehicle was struck by an IED.

NOTES:

Erin

15 Split Clean 40lb Dumbbells

21 Pull-ups

5 rounds for time

Canadian Army Master Corporal Erin Doyle, 32, was killed in a firefight August 11th, 2008 in the Panjwaii District, Kandahar Province, Afghanistan.

NOTES:

Falkel

8 Handstand Push-ups

8 Box Jump 30" box

15 ft Rope Climb 1 ascent

As Many Rounds As Possible in 25 Minutes

U.S. Army Staff Sergeant Chris Falkel, 22, of Highlands Ranch, CO, assigned to the 1st Battalion, 3rd Special Forces Group, based in Fort Bragg, NC, was killed on August 8, 2005 by enemy small-arms fire in Deh Afghan, Afghanistan.

NOTES:

Feeks

Shuttle Sprints 100m

**Squat Clean Thrusters
65lbs/29kg dumbbells**

Complete as many reps as possible in 7 minutes following the rep scheme below:

Round 1: 2 Shuttle Sprint, 2 Squat Clean Thrusters
Round 2: 4 Shuttle Sprint, 4 Squat Clean Thrusters
Round 3: 6 Shuttle Sprint, 6 Squat Clean Thrusters
Round 4: 8 Shuttle Sprint, 8 Squat Clean Thrusters
Round 5: 10 Shuttle Sprint, 10 Squat Clean Thrusters
Round 6: 12 Shuttle Sprint, 12 Squat Clean Thrusters
Round 7: 14 Shuttle Sprint, 14 Squat Clean Thrusters
Round 8: 16 Shuttle Sprint, 16 Squat Clean Thrusters

For time

Special Warfare Operator Petty Officer 1st Class Patrick D. Feeks, 28, of Edgewater, MD, assigned to a Naval Special Warfare unit based on the West Coast, died Aug. 16, 2012, in a helicopter crash northeast of Kandahar, Afghanistan, while supporting Operation Enduring Freedom.

NOTES:

Foo

13 Bench Press
170lbs/77kg

Then, complete as many rounds as possible in 20 minutes o

7 Chest to bar Pull-ups

77 Double Unders

2 Squat Clean Thrusters
170lbs/77kg

28 Sit-ups

20 min AMRAP, with buy-in

Sgt. Gary "Foo" Morales, of the Port St. Lucie County Sheriff's Office in Florida, died Feb. 28, 2013. Morales, 35, was fatally shot during a traffic stop. The Air Force veteran was employed by the St. Lucie County Sherriff's Office for 12 years and had just been promoted to Sergeant Deputy.

NOTES:

Forrest

20 L Pull-ups

30 Toes to bar

40 Burpees

800 meter Run

3 rounds for time

U.S. Drug Enforcement Administration Special Agent Forrest Nelson Leamon, 37, assigned to the Foreign-deployed Advisory and Support Team (FAST) Echo was killed October 26th, 2009, while on a counternarcotics mission in Western Afghanistan when the helicopter he was in crashed

NOTES:

Gallant

1 mile Run with a 20 lbs medicine ball

60 Burpee Pull-ups

800 meter Run with a 20 lbs medicine ball

30 Burpee Pull-ups

400 meter Run with a 20 lbs medicine ball

15 Burpee Pull-ups

For time

U.S. Navy Petty Officer Second Class Taylor Gallant, 22, of Winchester, KY, assigned to the Explosive Ordnance Disposal Mobile Unit 12, based in Joint Expeditionary Base Little Creek in Virginia Beach, VA, died on January 26, 2012, while conducting diving operations off the North Carolina coast in the Atlantic Ocean.

NOTES:

Garrett

75 Squats

25 Ring Handstand Push-up

25 L Pull-ups

3 rounds for time

Marine Capt. Garrett T. "Tubes" Lawton, 31, of Charleston, West Virginia was killed by an IED strike in Herat Province, Afghanistan on August 4, 2008.

NOTES:

Gator

5 Front Squat 185lbs

26 Ring Push-ups

8 rounds for time

U.S. Army Specialist Christopher "Gator" Gathercole, 21, of Santa Rosa, CA, assigned to 2nd Battalion, 75th RangerRegiment, based in Fort Lewis, WA, was killed by enemy fire on May 26, 2008, in Ghazni, Afghanistan.

NOTES:

Gaza

35 Kettlebell Swing
1.5 pood (apx 55lbs)

30 Push-ups

25 Pull-ups

20 Box Jump 30" box

1 mile Run

5 rounds for time

U.S. Air Force Major Lucas "Gaza" Gruenther, of Twain Harte, California, died Jan. 28, 2013, when his F-16 jet went down in the Adriatic Sea off the coast of Italy. Gruenther was in the 555th Fighter Squadron where he served as an F-16 Flight Lead for the 31st Fighter Wing, Aviano Air Base, Italy.

NOTES:

Glen

30 Clean and Jerk
(M=135lbs, F=95lbs)

1 mile Run

15 ft Rope Climb
10 ascents

1 mile Run

100 Burpees

For time

Former U.S. Navy SEAL Glen Doherty, 42, of Winchester, MA, assigned to a State Department security detail in Benghazi, Libya, died in an attack on a U.S. consulate on September 11, 2012.

NOTES:

Griff

1. 800 meter Run
2. 400 meter Run backwards

3. 800 meter Run
4. 400 meter Run backwards

For time

In honor of USAF SSgt Travis L. Griffin, 28, who was killed April 3, 2008 in the Rasheed district of Baghdad by an IED strike to his vehicle.

NOTES:

Hall

1. 3 Cleans 225lbs/102kg

2. 200 meters Sprint

3. 20 Kettlebell Snatches
10 reps each arm, 1.5 pood

4. 2 min Rest

5 rounds for time

U.S. Air Force Capt. Ryan P. Hall, of Colorado Springs, Colorado, died Feb. 18, 2012, near Camp Lemonnier, Djibouti, Africa, when his single-engine U-28 aircraft crashed. There were four total fatalities. The 30-year-old was assigned to the 319th Special Operations Squadron, Hurlburt Field, Florida.

NOTES:

Hamilton

1000 meter Row

50 Push-ups

1000 meter Run

50 Pull-ups

3 rounds for time

U.S. Army Specialist Adam Hamilton, 22, of Kent, OH, assigned to the 4th Squadron, 4th Cavalry Regiment, 1st Brigade Combat Team, 1st Infantry Division, based in Fort Riley, KS, died on May, 28, 2011 in Haji Ruf, Afghanistan, of wounds suffered when enemy forces attacked his unit with an improvised explosive device.

NOTES:

Hammer

5 Power Clean
(M=135lbs, F=95lbs)

10 Front Squat
(M=135lbs, F=95lbs)

5 Jerk
(M=135lbs, F=95lbs)

20 Pull-ups

5 rounds - Each Round for time
Rest 90 seconds between each round

U.S. Army First Sergeant Michael "Hammer" Bordelon, 37, of Morgan City, LA, assigned to the 1st Battalion, 24th Infantry Regiment, 1st Brigade, 25th Infantry Division (Stryker Brigade Combat Team), based out of Fort Lewis, WA, died on May 10, 2005, from injuries sustained when a car bomb exploded near him in Mosul, Iraq on April 23, 2005.

NOTES:

Hansen

30 Kettlebell Swing
2 pood (apx 70lbs)

30 Burpees

30 Glute-Ham Sit-Ups

5 rounds for time

Marine Staff Sgt Daniel Hansen died February 14th in Farah Providence, Afghanistan when an IED he was working on detonated.

NOTES:

Harper

9 Chest to bar Pull-ups

15 Power Cleans
135lbs/61kg

21 Squats

400 meter Run
with a 45lbs/20kg plate

23 min AMRAP

Phoenix Firefighter Brad Harper, 23, of Peoria, Arizona, died while on the scene of a two-alarm fire on May 19, 2013. Harper loved being a firefighter and had worked with the Phoenix Fire Department, where he was assigned to Rescue 21, for two years.

NOTES:

Helton

800 meter Run

30 Squat Clean
50lb Dumbbells

30 Burpees

3 rounds for time

U.S. Air Force Security Forces 1st Lt. Joseph D. Helton, 24, of Monroe, GA, assigned to the 6th Security Forces Squadron at MacDill Air Force Base in Tampa, FL, was killed September 8th, 2009, while on a mission near Baghdad, Iraq, when an improvised explosive device detonated near his vehicle.

NOTES:

Hidalgo

1. 2 mile Run

2. 2 minutes Rest

3. 20 Squat Clean (M=135lbs, F=95lbs)

4. 20 Box Jump 24"

5. 20 Walking Lunge steps with 45lb plate held overhead

6. 20 Box Jump 24"

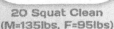
7. 20 Squat Clean (M=135lbs, F=95lbs)

8. 2 minutes Rest

9. 2 mile Run

For time
If you've got a twenty pound vest or body armor, wear it.

U.S. Army First Lieutenant Daren M. Hidalgo, 24, of Waukesha, WI, assigned to 3rd Squadron, 2nd Stryker Cavalry Regiment, based in Vilseck, Germany, died on February 20, 2011, in Kandahar province, Afghanistan, from wounds suffered when insurgents attacked his unit with an improvised explosive device. Two weeks prior to his death, he was hit by an earlier improvised explosive device. Despite his injuries, he stayed in country and on patrols rather than return home.

Holbrook

5 Thrusters
(M=115lbs. F=80lbs)

10 Pull-ups

100 meter Sprint

10 Rounds – time each round
Rest 1 minute between each round

US Army Captain Jason Holbrook, 28, of Burnet, TX, assigned to 1st Battalion, 3rd Special Forces Group (Airborne), based out of Fort Bragg, NC, was killed on July 29th, 2010 in Tsagay, Afghanistan when insurgents attacked his vehicle with an improvised explosive device.

NOTES:

Holleyman

5 Wallballs

3 Handstand Push-ups

1 Power Clean 225lbs

30 rounds for time

U.S. Army Staff Sergeant Aaron N. Holleyman, 27, of Glasgow, MS, assigned to the 1st Battalion, 5th Special Forces Group, based in Fort Campbell, KY, was killed on August 30, 2004, when his military vehicle hit an improvised explosive device in Khutayiah, Iraq.

NOTES:

Hortman

800 meter Run

80 Squats

8 Muscle-ups

As Many Rounds As Possible in 45 Minutes

U.S. Army Captain John D. Hortman, 30, of Inman, SC, assigned to the 1st Battalion, 160th Special Operations Aviation Regiment, based in Fort Campbell, KY, died on August 8, 2011, in Fort Benning, GA, in a helicopter accident during a military training exercise

NOTES:

Horton

9 Bar Muscle-ups

11 Clean and Jerks
155lbs/70kg

50 yards Buddy carry

9 rounds for time, with a partner

Share the work with your partner however you choose with only one person working at a time. If you can't find a partner perform 5 reps of each exercise per round and find a heavy sandbag to carry.

U.S. Army Spc. Christopher D. Horton, of Collinsville, Oklahoma, died Sept. 9, 2011, in Zurmat District, Afghanistan, of wounds sustained when enemy forces attacked his unit with small-arms fire. The 26-year old was assigned to 1st Battalion, 279 Infantry Regiment, 45th Infantry Brigade Combat Team, Oklahoma National Guard.

NOTES:

Jack

10 Push Press
(M=115lbs. F=80lbs)

10 Kettlebell Swing
1.5 pood (apx 55lbs)

10 Box Jump 24"

**As Many Rounds As Possible
in 20 minutes**

Army Staff Sgt. Jack M. Martin III, 26, of Bethany, OK, assigned to the 3rd Battalion, 1st Special Forces Group, Fort Lewis, WA, died September 29th, 2009, in Jolo Island, Philippines, from the detonation of an improvised explosive device.

NOTES:

Jag 28

800 meter Run

28 Kettlebell Swings
2 pood (apx 72lbs)

28 Strict Pull-ups

28 Kettlebell Clean and Jerk
2 pood each

28 Strict Pull-ups

800 meter Run

For time

U.S. Air Force Senior Airman Mark Forester, 29, of Tuscaloosa, AL, assigned to the 21st Special Tactics Squadron, based in Pope Air Force Base, NC, died on September 29, 2010, while conducting combat operations in Uruzgan province, Afghanistan.

NOTES:

Jared

800 meter Run

40 Pull-ups

70 Push-ups

4 rounds for time

U.S. Army Master Sergeant Jared N. Van Aalst, 34, of Laconia, NH, assigned to the U.S. Army Special Operations Command, based in Fort Bragg, NC, died August 4, 2010, in Kunduz province, Afghanistan, of wounds suffered while his unit was conducting combat operations.

NOTES:

Jason

100 Squats

5 Muscle-ups

75 Squats

10 Muscle-ups

50 Squats

15 Muscle-ups

25 Squats

20 Muscle-ups

For time

S01 (SEAL) Jason Dale Lewis was killed by an IED while conducting combat operations in Southern Baghdad July 6, 2007.

NOTES:

JBO

9 Overhead squats
115lbs/52kg

15ft Legless Rope Climb
1 ascent (beginning from seated)

12 Bench Presses
115lbs/52kg

As Many Rounds and Reps As Possible in 28 minutes

U.S. Army Staff Sgt. Jeremie "JBo" "Bubba" Border, 28, of Mesquite, TX, assigned to the 1st Battalion, 1st Special Forces Group (Airborne), based in Torii Station, Okinawa, Japan, died Sept. 1, 2012, in Batur Village, Afghanistan, from wounds suffered when enemy forces attacked his unit with small-arms fire.

NOTES:

Jennifer

10 Pull-ups

**15 Kettlebell Swings
1.5 pood (apx 55lbs)**

20 Box jumps 24" box

26 min AMRAP

Canadian 1st Class Constable Jennifer Kovach of Guelph, Canada, died March 14, 2013, when her squad car was involved in a motor-vehicle accident while she was responding to a call for service. The 26-year-old fulfilled her dream of becoming a police officer serving her community and the Guelph Police Service for four years before her death.

NOTES:

Jenny

20 Overhead squats
45lbs/20kg

20 Back Squats
45lbs/20kg

400 meters Run

20 min AMRAP

U.S. Army Capt. Jennifer M. Moreno, of San Diego, California, died Oct. 6, 2013, in Zhari District, Afghanistan, when enemy forces attacked her unit with an improvised explosive device. The 25-year-old was assigned to Madigan Army Medical Center on Joint Base Lewis-McChord in Washington state.

NOTES:

Jerry

1 mile Run

2000 meter Row

1 mile Run

For time

Sgt Major Jerry Dwayne Patton, 40, died on 15 October 2008 during High Altitude High Opening (HAHO) training while assigned to Army USSOCOM preparing for deployment to Afghanistan.

NOTES:

J.J.

1. Squat Clean 185lbs

2. Parallette Handstand Push-ups

Round 1: 1 Squat Clean 185lbs, 10 Parallette Handstand Push-ups
Round 2: 2 Squat Clean 185lbs, 9 Parallette Handstand Push-ups
Round 3: 3 Squat Clean 185lbs, 8 Parallette Handstand Push-ups
Round 4: 4 Squat Clean 185lbs, 7 Parallette Handstand Push-ups
Round 5: 5 Squat Clean 185lbs, 6 Parallette Handstand Push-ups
Round 6: 6 Squat Clean 185lbs, 5 Parallette Handstand Push-ups
Round 7: 7 Squat Clean 185lbs, 4 Parallette Handstand Push-ups
Round 8: 8 Squat Clean 185lbs, 3 Parallette Handstand Push-ups
Round 9: 9 Squat Clean 185lbs, 2 Parallette Handstand Push-ups
Round 10: 10 Squat Clean 185lbs, 1 Parallette Handstand Push-ups

For Time

U.S. Marine Lance Corporal Justin James "JJ" Wilson, 24, of Palm City, FL, assigned to 3rd Battalion, 10th Marine Regiment, 2nd Marine Division, II Marine Expeditionary Force, based in Camp Lejeune, NC, was killed on March 22, 2010, while supporting combat operations in Helmand province, Afghanistan.

NOTES:

John Rankel

6 Deadlift 225lbs

7 Burpee Pull-ups

**10 Kettlebell Swings
2 pood (apx 72lbs)**

200 meter Run

As Many Rounds As Possible
in 20 minutes

U.S. Marine Corps Sergeant John Rankel, 23, of Speedway, IN, assigned to 3d Battalion, 1st Marine Regiment, 1st Marine Division, 1 Marine Expeditionary Force, based out of Camp Pendleton, CA, was killed on June 7, 2010, while supporting combat operations in Helmand Province, Afghanistan.

NOTES:

Johnson

9 Deadlift 245lbs

8 Muscle-ups

9 Squat Cleans 155lbs

As Many Rounds As Possible in 20 minutes

1st Lt. Michael E. Johnson, 25, of the U.S. Marine Corps 7th Communications Battalion, 3rd Marine Headquarters Group, III Marine Expeditionary Force, headquartered in Okinawa, Japan, died September 8, 2009 while supporting combat operations in Kunar province, Afghanistan.

NOTES:

Jorge

1. 30 GHD Sit-ups

2. 15 Squat Clean 155lbs

3. 24 GHD Sit-ups

4. 12 Squat Clean 155lbs

5. 18 GHD Sit-ups

6. 9 Squat Clean 155lbs

7. 12 GHD Sit-ups

8. 6 Squat Clean 155lbs

9. 6 GHD Sit-ups

10. 3 Squat Clean 155lbs

For time

U.S. Coast Guard Chief Petty Officer Fernando Jorge, 39, of Cypress, CA, an Aviation Survival Technician Chief, died on February 28, 2012, when his unit's helicopter crashed into Mobile Bay in the Gulf of Mexico during a training mission.

NOTES:

Josh

1. 21 Overhead Squats (M=95lbs. F=65lbs)
2. 42 Pull-ups
3. 15 Overhead Squats (M=95lbs. F=65lbs)
4. 30 Pull-ups
5. 9 Overhead Squats (M=95lbs. F=65lbs)
6. 18 Pull-ups

For time

SSG Joshua Hager, United States Army, was killed Thursday February 22 2007 in Ar Ramadi, Iraq.

NOTES:

Joshie

21 Right arm Snatch 40lb Dumbbell

21 L Pull-ups

21 Left arm Snatch 40lb Dumbbell

21 L Pull-ups

3 rounds for time
The snatches are full squat snatches

In honor of Army Staff Sergeant Joshua Whitaker, 23, of Long Beach, CA who was killed in Afghanistan May 15th, 2007.

NOTES:

JT

Handstand Push-ups

Ring Dips

Push-ups

21-15-9 reps for time

In honor of Petty Officer 1st Class Jeff Taylor, 30, of Little Creek, VA, who was killed in Afghanistan June 2005

NOTES:

Justin

Body-weight back squats   Body-weight bench press

Strict pull-ups

30-20-10 Reps for Time

U.S. Marine Corps Sgt. Justin M. Hansen, 26, of Traverse City, Michigan--assigned to the 2nd Marine Special Operations Battalion, based in Camp Lejeune, North Carolina--died July 24, 2012, in Badghis Province, Afghanistan, while conducting combat operations.

NOTES:

Kevin

32 Deadlifts
185lbs/83kg

32 Hanging Hip Touches
(Alternating arms)

800 meters Farmer carry
15lbs/6kg Dumbbells

3 Rounds For Time

Navy Special Warfare Operator 1st Class Kevin Ebbert, 32, of Arcata, CA, assigned to an East Coast-based Naval Special Warfare unit in Virginia Beach, VA, died Nov. 24, 2012 in Uruzgan Province, Afghanistan, while supporting combat stability operations.

NOTES:

Klepto

27 Box Jumps 24"

20 Burpees

11 Squat Cleans 145lbs

4 rounds for time

U.S. Air Force Major David "Klepto" L. Brodeur, 34, of Auburn, MA, assigned to the 11th Air Force, based at Joint Base Elmendorf-Richardson, AK, died on April 27, 2011 in Kabul, Afghanistan, of wounds sustained from gunfire from an Afghan military trainee.

NOTES:

Kutschbach

11 Back Squats
185lbs/83kg

10 Jerks
135lbs/61kg

7 rounds for time

U.S. Army Staff Sgt. Patrick Kutschbach, of McKees Rocks, Pennsylvania, died Nov. 10, 2007, in Bagram, Afghanistan, from injuries sustained when his vehicle was hit by a rocket-propelled grenade and small-arms fire in Tagab Valley, Afghanistan. The 25-year-old was assigned to the 1st Battalion, 10th Special Forces Group in Germany.

NOTES:

Ledesma

5 Parallette Handstand Push-ups

10 Toes through Rings

15 Medicine Ball Cleans 20lbs

As Many Rounds As Possible
in 20 minutes

Narcotics Detective and Special Assignment Unit Operator Carlos Ledesma, 34, of the Chandler Police Department, Chandler, AZ, was shot and killed by drug dealers on July 28, 2010, during an undercover operation in Phoenix, AZ.

NOTES:

Lee

400 meter Run

1 Deadlift 345lbs

3 Squat Clean 185lbs

5 Push Jerk 185lbs

3 Muscle-ups

15 Ft Rope climb
1 ascent

5 rounds for time

U.S. Army Staff Sergeant Dick Alson Lee Jr., 31, of Orange Park, Florida, assigned to the 95th Military Police Battalion, 18th Military Police Brigade, 21st Theater Sustainment Command, based in Sembach, Germany, died on April 26, 2012 from injuries sustained when his vehicle encountered an improvised explosive device in Ghazni province, Afghanistan.

NOTES:

Loredo

24 Squats

24 Push-ups

24 Steps Walking Lunge

400 meter Run

6 rounds for time

U.S. Army Staff Sergeant Edwardo Loredo, 34, of Houston, TX, assigned to the 2nd Battalion, 508th Parachute Infantry Regiment, 4th Brigade Combat Team, 82d Airborne Division, based in Fort Bragg, N was killed on June 24, 2010 in Jelewar, Afghanistan, when insurgents attacked his unit with an improvis explosive device.

NOTES:

Luce

1000 meter Run

10 Muscle-ups

100 Squats

3 rounds for time
Wearing a 20lbs vest

Captain Ronald G. Luce, 27, of the U.S. Army Company C, 2nd Battalion, 20th Special Forces Group, headquartered at Jackson, MS, died August 2, 2009 in Qole Gerdsar, Afghanistan, after his vehicle was struck by a command wire improvised explosive device.

NOTES:

Luke

400 meters Run

15 Clean and Jerk
155lbs/70kg

400 meters Run

30 Toes to bar

400 meters Run

45 Wallballs
20lbs/9kg

400 meters Run

45 Kettlebell Swings
1.5 pood (apx 55lbs)

400 meters Run

30 Ring dips

400 meters Run

15 Steps Weighted Lunge
155lbs/70kg

400 meters Run

For time

Marine Staff Sgt. Leon H. Lucas Jr. died Aug. 1, 2011, in Helmand Province, Afghanistan, of injuries sustained from an enemy grenade attack in the upper Gereshk Valley. The 32-year-old, of Wilson, North Carolina, was assigned to the 3rd Battalion, 4th Marine Regiment, Twentynine Palms, California, and served during Operation Enduring Freedom.

NOTES:

Manion

400 meter Run

29 Back Squat
(M=135lbs, F=95lbs)

7 rounds for time

First Lieutenant Travis Manion, 26, of Doylestown, PA, assigned to 1st Reconnaissance Battalion, 1st Marine Division, I Marine Expeditionary Force, based in Camp Pendleton, CA, was killed by sniper fire on April 29, 2007 while fighting against an enemy ambush in Anbar Province, Iraq.

NOTES:

Marco

21 Pull-ups

15 Handstand Push-ups

9 Thrusters
135lbs/61kg

3 rounds for time

U.S. Marine Cpl. Marc T. Ryan, of Gloucester City, New Jersey, died Nov. 15, 2004, from a roadside bomb in Ramadi, Iraq. The 25-year-old was a weapons specialist assigned to the 2nd Battalion, 5th Marine Regiment, 1st Marine Division, I Marine Expeditionary Force at the Marine Corps Base Camp in Pendleton, California.

NOTES:

Matt 16

16 Deadlifts
275lbs/124kg

16 Hang Power Cleans
185lbs/83kg

16 Push Press
135lbs/61kg

800 meters Run

4 rounds for time

U.S. Army Chief Warrant Officer Matt Ruffner, of Tafford, Pennsylvania, died April 9, 2013, in Pachir Wa Agam district, Afghanistan, from injuries sustained when his AH-64 Apache helicopter crashed. The 34-year-old was assigned to 1st Attack Reconnaissance Battalion, 104th Aviation Regiment, 28th Combat Aviation Brigade, 28th Infantry Division, Pennsylvania National Guard, Fort Indiantown Gap, Pennsylvania.

NOTES:

McCluskey

9 Muscle-ups

15 Burpee Pull-ups

21 Pull-ups

800 meter Run

3 rounds for time

U.S. Army Sergeant Jason "Mick" McCluskey, 26, of McAlester, OK, assigned to the 27th Engineer Battalion, 20th Engineer Brigade, XVIII Airborne Corps, based out of Fort Bragg, NC, was killed on November 4, 2010, when insurgents attacked his unit with small arms fire in Zarghun Shahr, Mohammad Agha district, Afghanistan.

NOTES:

McGhee

5 Deadlift 275lbs

13 Push-ups

9 Box Jump 24" box

As Many Rounds as Possible in 30 minutes

Corporal Ryan C. McGhee, 21, was killed in action on May 13, 2009 by small arms fire during combat in central Iraq. He served with 3rd Battalion, 75th Ranger Regiment of Fort Benning, Ga. This was his fourth deployment, his first to Iraq.

NOTES:

Meadows

20 Muscle-ups

25 Lowers from an inverted hang on the rings, slowly, with straight body and arms

30 Ring Handstand Push-ups

35 Ring Rows

40 Ring Push-ups

For time

U.S. Marine Corps Captain Joshua S. Meadows, 30, of Bastrop, TX, assigned to 1st Marine Special Operations Battalion, Marine Corps Forces Special Operations Command, based in Camp Pendleton, CA was killed by enemy fire on September 5, 2009 in Farah Province, Afghanistan.

NOTES:

Michael

800 meter Run

50 Back Extensions

50 Sit-ups

3 rounds for time

In honor of Navy Lieutenant Michael McGreevy, 30, of Portville, NY, who was killed in Afghanistan June 28 2005

NOTES:

Moon

10 Right arm Hang Split Snatch 40lb Dumbbell

15 ft Rope Climb 1 ascent

10 Left arm Hang Split Snatch 40lb Dumbbell

15 ft Rope Climb 1 ascent

7 rounds for time
Alternate feet in the split snatch sets.

Moon, 20, of Tucson, AZ, assigned to 2d Battalion, 508th Parachute Infantry Regiment, 4th Brigade Combat Team, 82nd Airborne Division, based out of Fort Bragg, NC, died on July 13, 2010, from injuries sustained on July 6, 2010 in Arghandab, Afghanistan when insurgents attacked his vehicle with an improvised explosive device.

NOTES:

Moore

15 ft Rope Climb 1 ascent

400 meter Run

Max rep Handstand Push-ups

As Many Rounds As Possible in 20 minutes

Officer David S. Moore, 29, of the Indianapolis Metropolitan Police Department, died on January 26, 2011 from gunshot wounds suffered on January 23, 2011 when he stopped a stolen vehicle and the driver opened fire at him.

NOTES:

Morrison

Wallballs

Box jump 24"

Kettlebell Swings
1.5 pood (apx 55lbs)

50, 40, 30, 20, 10 reps per round for time

U.S. Army Specialist Scott Morrison, 23, of Blue Ash, OH, assigned to 584th Mobility Augmentation Company, 20th Engineer Battalion, 36th Engineer Brigade, based out of Fort Hood, TX, died on September 26, 2010, from injuries suffered on September 25 when insurgents in Kandahar, Afghanistan attacked his vehicle with an improvised explosive device.

NOTES:

Mr Joshua

1. 400 meter Run

2. 30 Glute-Ham Sit-Ups

3. 15 Deadlift 250lbs

5 rounds for time

SO1 Joshua Thomas Harris, 36, drowned during combat operations, August 30th 2008 in Afghanistan.

NOTES:

Murph

1 mile Run

100 Pull-ups

200 Push-ups

300 Squats

1 mile Run

For time

In memory of Navy Lieutenant Michael Murphy, 29, of Patchogue, N.Y., who was killed in Afghanistan June 28th, 2005.

NOTES:

Nate

2 Muscle-ups

4 Handstand Push-ups

8 Kettlebell Swings 2 pood (apx 72lbs)

As Many Rounds As Possible in 20 minutes

In honor of Chief Petty Officer Nate Hardy, who was killed Sunday February 4th during combat operations in Iraq.

NOTES:

Ned

11 Body Weight Back Squats

1000 meters Row

7 Rounds For Time

Special Agent Nathan "Ned" Schuldheiss, 27, of Newport, RI, a civilian assigned to the Air Force Office of Special Investigations, Detachment 204 Offutt Air Force Base, NE, died Nov. 1, 2007 near Balad Air Base, Iraq, of wounds sustained from an improvised-explosive device that struck his vehicle. .

NOTES:

Nick

**10 Hang Squat Clean
45 pound Dumbbells**

**6 Handstand Push-ups
on Dumbbells**

12 rounds for time

U.S. Army Specialist Nicholas P. Steinbacher, 22, of La Crescenta, CA, assigned to the 2nd Battalion, 5th Cavalry Regiment, 1st Brigade, 1st Cavalry Division, based in Fort Hood, TX, died on December 10, 2006 of injuries suffered when insurgents attacked his Humvee with an improvised explosive device in Baghdad, Iraq.

NOTES:

Nukes

8 minutes to complete:

1 mile Run

Deadlifts
max reps 315lbs

Then, 10 minutes to complete:

1 mile Run

Power Cleans
max reps 225lbs

Then, 12 minutes to complete:

1 mile Run

Overhead Squats
max reps 135lbs

Do not rest between rounds.
Post run times and reps
completed for each exercise.

U.S. Marine Corps Capt. Matthew "Nukes" Manoukian, 29, of Los Altos Hills, Calif., assigned to the 1st Marine Special Operations Battalion, based in Camp Pendleton, Calif., died Aug. 10, 2012, in Sangin District, Afghanistan, after being shot by an Afghan policeman.

NOTES:

Nutts

10 Handstand Push-ups

15 Deadlift 250lbs

25 Box Jumps, 30" Box

50 Pull-ups

100 Wallballs

200 Double Unders

400 meter Run with a 45lb plate

For time

Lieutenant Andrew Richard Nuttall, 30, from the 1st Battalion Princess Patricia's Canadian Light Infantry (1 PPCLI), based in Edmonton, Alberta, serving as a memberof the 1 PPCLI Battle Group was killed by an improvised explosive device that detonated during a joint foot patrol near the village of Nakhonay in Panjwaii District, about 25 km southwest of Kandahar City on December 23, 2009

NOTES:

Omar

1. 10 Thrusters (M=95lbs. F=65lbs)
2. 15 Bar-facing burpees
3. 20 Thrusters (M=95lbs. F=65lbs)
4. 25 Bar-facing burpees
5. 30 Thrusters (M=95lbs. F=65lbs)
6. 35 Bar-facing burpees

For time

U.S. Army First Lieutenant Omar Vazquez, 25, of Hamilton, NJ, assigned to the 2d Squadron, 3rd Armored Cavalry Regiment, based in Fort Hood, TX, died of wounds suffered April 22, 2011, when insurgents in Numaniyah, Iraq, attacked his unit with an improvised explosive device.

NOTES:

Ozzy

11 Deficit Handstand Push-ups

1000 meters Run

7 Rounds For Time

U.S. Air Force Master Sgt. Thomas "Ozzy" Crowell, 36, of Neosho, MO, died Nov. 1, 2007, near Balad Air Base in Iraq. The special agent for the Air Force Office of Special Investigations, Detachment 301 at Scott Air Force Base, Il sustained wounds from an improvised explosive device that struck his vehicle. .

NOTES:

Paul

50 Double Unders

35 Knees to Elbows

Overhead Walk 20 yards 185lbs

5 rounds for time

Pittsburgh Police Officer Paul John Rizzo Domenic Sciullo II, 36, was shot and killed in the line of duty while responding to a domestic disturbance call on April 4, 2009.

NOTES:

Pheezy

5 Front Squat 165lbs

18 Pull-ups

5 Deadlift 225lbs

18 Toes to Bar

5 Push Jerk 165lbs

18 Hand Release Push-ups

3 rounds for time

U.S. Marine Corps Lance Corporal Philip P. Clark, 19, of Gainesville, FL, assigned to 1st Battalion, 6th Marine Regiment, 2nd Marine Division, II Marine Expeditionary Force, based in Camp Lejeune, NC, died on May 18, 2010, while supporting combat operations in Helmand province, Afghanistan

NOTES:

Pike

20 Thrusters
75lbs/34kg

10 Strict Ring dips

20 Push-ups

10 Strict Handstand Push-ups

50 meters Bear crawl

5 rounds for time

U.S. Navy Chief Petty Officer Christian Michael Pike, of Peoria, Arizona, died March 12, 2013, in Landstuhl, Germany. Pike, 31, sustained combat-related injuries days earlier while conducting stability operations in the Maiwand District of Kandahar, Afghanistan. He was assigned to the West Coast-based Naval Special Warfare unit in California. The Chief Cryptologic Technician was posthumously awarded the Bronze Star with Valor.

NOTES:

PK

10 Back Squats
225lbs/102kg

10 Deadlifts
275lbs/124kg

400 meters Sprint

2 min Rest

5 rounds for time

U.S. Army Capt. Andrew Pedersen-Keel, of South Miami, Florida, died March 11, 2013. The 28-year-old was assigned to 1st Battalion, 3rd Special Forces Group (Airborne), in Fort Bragg, North Carolina. Pedersen-Keel was fatally injured in Jalrez District, Afghanistan, from small-arms fire from an Afghan security-forces member.

NOTES:

Rahoi

12 Box Jumps 24"

**6 Thruster
(M=95lbs, F=65lbs)**

6 Bar-facing Burpees

As Many Rounds As Possible in 12 minutes

U.S. FBI Supervisory Special Agent Gregory J. Rahoi, 38, of Brookfield, WI, assigned to the Hostage Rescue Team, based in Quantico, VA, was killed on December 6, 2006, during a live-fire tactical training exercise at Fort A.P. Hill, near Bowling Green, VA.

NOTES:

Ralph

8 Deadlift 250lbs

16 Burpees

**15 ft Rope Climb
3 ascents**

600 meter Run

4 rounds for time

British Army Second Lieutenant Ralph Johnson, 24, of South Africa, assigned to the Household Cavalry Regiment, based in Windsor, England, was killed on August 1, 2006, in Helmand province, Afghanistan, when insurgents attacked his vehicle with an improvised explosive device.

NOTES:

Randy

75 Power Snatch
(M=75lbs. F=50/55lbs)

For time

In honor of Randy Simmons, 51, a 27 year LAPD veteran and SWAT team member who was killed February 6 in the line of duty.

NOTES:

René

400 meters Run

21 Steps Walking Lunge

15 Pull-ups

9 Burpees

7 rounds for time
If you have a 20lbs/9kg vest or body armor, wear it.

Danish Army Sgt. René Brink Jakobsen of Vang, Denmark, died Jan. 3, 2013, after being hit by an improvised explosive device while on foot patrol with his unit in Upper Gereshk Valley in Helmand Province, Afghanistan. The 39-year-old was a member of the elite Danish Special Forces Ranger unit called Jaegerkorpet.

NOTES:

Ricky

10 Pull-ups

**5 Deadlift
75lb Dumbbells**

**8 Push Press
(M=135lbs, F=95lbs)
As Many Rounds As Possible
in 20 minutes**

U.S. Army Sergeant William "Ricky" Rudd, 27, of Madisonville, KY, assigned to the 3rd Battalion, 75th Ranger Regiment, based in Fort Benning, GA, died on October 5, 2008, from wounds suffered from enemy small arms fire while on a combat patrol in Mosul, Iraq.

NOTES:

Riley

1.5 miles Run

150 Burpees

1.5 miles Run

For time
If you've got a weight vest or body armor, wear it.

Army Sgt. 1st Class Riley G. Stephens, 39, of Tolar, Texas, assigned to the 1st Battalion, 3rd Special Forces Group (Airborne), died Sept. 28, 2012, in Wardak, Afghanistan, of wounds caused by enemy small-arms fire.

NOTES:

RJ

800 meter Run

**15 ft Rope Climb
5 ascents**

50 Push-ups

5 rounds for time

Veteran LAPD officer and United States Marine Corps Reservist Sergeant Major Robert J Cottle, 45, was killed by an improvised explosive device while on patrol in Southern Afghanistan on Wednesday, March 24, 2010. RJ joined theMarines at age 18, and the LAPD in 1990. His various LAPD assignments include Hollywood Vice, Southeast Area, LAPD Dive Team and, most recently, SWAT.

NOTES:

Robbie

8 Handstand Push-ups

**15ft L-sit Rope climb
1 ascent**

25 min AMRAP

U.S. Army Staff Sergeant Robert J. Miller died Jan. 25, 2008, in Bari Kowt, Afghanistan, of wounds sustained when he encountered small-arms fire while conducting combat operations. The 24-year-old, of Oviedo, Florida, was assigned to the 3rd Battalion, 3rd Special Forces Group (Airborne) in Fort Bragg, North Carolina, and served during Operation Enduring Freedom. In October of 2010, Miller was awarded the Medal of Honor posthumously for his heroic actions in combat.

NOTES:

Rocket

50 yards Swim

10 Push-ups

15 Squats

As Many Rounds and Reps As Possible in 30 minutes

Army Sgt. 1st Class Aaron "Rocket" Henderson, 33, of Houlton, Maine, assigned to the 2nd Battalion, 5th Special Forces Group (Airborne), died Oct. 2, 2012, at Bagram Air Base, Afghanistan, of wounds suffered from an improvised explosive device in Zombalay Village, Afghanistan.

NOTES:

Roney

200 meter Run

11 Thruster
(M=135lbs, F=95lbs)

200 meter Run

11 Push Press
(M=135lbs, F=95lbs)

200 meter Run

11 Bench Press
(M=135lbs, F=95lbs)

4 rounds for time

Police Service of Northern Ireland Constable Ronan Kerr, 25, of Omagh, Northern Ireland, was killed on April 2, 2011 by a car bomb outside his home in Omagh.

NOTES:

Roy

15 Deadlift 225lbs

20 Box Jumps 24"

25 Pull-ups

5 rounds for time

Marine Corps Sgt. Michael C. Roy, 25, of North Fort Myers, FL, assigned to the 3rd Marine Special Operations Battalion, Marine Special Operations Advisor Group, Marine Corps Forces Special Operations Command at Camp Lejeune, was killed in action on July 8th, 2009 in Nimroz Province, Afghanistan, while supporting combat operations.

NOTES:

Ryan

7 Muscle-ups

21 Burpees

5 rounds for time
Each burpee terminates with a jump
one foot above max standing reach

Maplewood, Missouri Firefighter, Ryan Hummert, 22, was killed by sniper fire July 21st 2008 when he stepped off his fire truck responding to a call.

NOTES:

Santiago

1. 18 Hang Squat Clean 35lb Dumbbells

2. 18 Pull-ups

3. 10 Power Clean (M=135lbs, F=95lbs)

4. 10 Handstand Push-ups

7 rounds for time

U.S. Army Sergeant Anibal Santiago, 37, of Belvidere, IL, assigned to the 3rd Battalion, 75th Ranger Regiment, stationed in Fort Benning, GA, died on July, 18, 2010, in Bagram, Afghanistan.

NOTES:

Santora

1 minute of Squat Cleans 155lbs

1 minute of 20' Shuttle Sprints
(20' forward + 20' backwards = 1 rep)

1 minute of Deadlifts 245lbs

1 minute of Burpees

1 minute of Jerks 155lbs

3 rounds for time
Rest 1 minute between each round

US Army Sergeant Jason A. Santora, of Farmingville, NY, assigned to the 3rd Battalion, 75th Ranger Regiment, based out of Fort Benning, GA died in Logar province, Afghanistan on April 23, 2010, from wounds sustained during a firefight with insurgents.

NOTES:

Scooter

On a 35 min clock with a partner, complete as many rounds as possible in 30 minutes of:

1. 30 Double Unders
2. 15 Pull-ups
3. 15 Push-ups
4. 100 meters Sprint

Then, 5 min to find a 1-rep-max Partner Deadlift.

Partner Deadlift

For the AMRAP, have one partner work while the other rests, switching after a full round is completed. If you're performing without a partner, rest 60 sec between each round, and find a regular 1-rep-max deadlift

30 min AMRAP, and 5 min to find 1-rep-max

Sgt. Scott Lunger, of Brentwood, California, died July 22, 2015, after being gunned down during a traffic stop. A second officer returned fire, hitting the suspect who was later caught and taken into police custody. Lunger, 48, had served the Hayward Police Department since 2001 as a beat cop, on the special duty unit, gang task force, SWAT, was a Field Training Officer and acting lieutenant at the time of his death.

NOTES:

Sean

11 Chest to Bar Pull-ups

**22 Front Squat
(M=75lbs, F=50/55lbs)**

10 rounds for time

U.S. Army Staff Sergeant Sean M. Flannery, 29, of Wyomissing, PA, assigned to the 2nd Battalion, 502nd Infantry Regiment, 2nd Brigade Combat Team, 101st Airborne Division (Air Assault), based in Fort Campbell, KY, was killed on November 22, 2010, in Kandahar province, Afghanistan, when insurgents attacked his unit with an improvised explosive device.

NOTES:

Servais

1.5 miles Run

Then, 8 rounds of:

19 Pull-ups

19 Push-ups

19 Burpees

Then:

400 meters
Sandbag carry (heavy)

1 mile Farmer carry
45lbs/20kg dumbells

For time

U.S. Air Force Senior Airman Adam Servais, of Onalaska, Wisconsin, died Aug. 19, 2006, in Uruzgan Province, Afghanistan, when his vehicle came under hostile fire. The 23-year-old was assigned to the 23r Special Tactics Squadron, Hurlburt Field, Florida.

NOTES:

Severin

50 Strict Pull-ups

100 Push-ups
release hands from floor at the bottom

5000 meter Run

For time
*If you've got a twenty pound vest
or body armor, wear it.

U.S. Army Sergeant First Class Severin W. Summers III, 43, of Bentonia, MS, assigned to the 2nd Battalion, 20th Special Forces Group (Airborne), headquartered at Jackson, MS, died August 2, 2009 in Qole Gerdsar, Afghanistan, after his vehicle was struck by a command wire improvised explosive device.

NOTES:

Sham

11 Body Weight Deadlifts

100 meters Sprint

7 Rounds For Time

Air Force Staff Sgt. David "Sham" Wieger, 28, of North Huntingdon, PA, a special agent for the Air Force of Special Investigations, Detachment 303, Travis Air Force Base, CA, died Nov. 1, 2007, near Balad Air Base, Iraq, of wounds sustained from an improvised explosive device that struck his vehicle.

NOTES:

Shawn

5 miles Run

50 Squats

50 Push-ups

Run in 5 minute intervals, stopping after each to perform 50 squats and 50 pushups before beginning the next 5 minute run interval.

For time and number of intervals

U.S. Army Captain Shawn G. Hogan, of Salem, New Hampshire, died Oct. 17, 2012. The 28-year-old was fatally injured in a training exercise at Land Between the Lakes National Recreation Area in Golden Pond, Kentucky. He was assigned to Company B, 4th Battalion, 5th Special Forces Group (Airborne) in Fort Campbell.

NOTES:

Ship

7 Squat Clean 185lbs

8 Burpee Box Jumps 36" box

9 rounds for time

Canadian Forces Sergeant Prescott Shipway, 36, of Esterhazy, SK, Canada, assigned to the 2nd Battalion, Princess Patricia's Canadian Light Infantry, based in Shilo, MB, Canada, was killed on September 7, 2008 by a roadside bomb in Kandahar province, Afghanistan.

NOTES:

Sisson

15 ft Rope Climb
1 ascent

5 Burpees

200 meters Run

20 min AMRAP
If you have a 20lbs/9kg vest or body armor, wear it.

U.S. Army 2nd Lt. Justin Sisson, 23, assigned to 1st Battalion, 506th Infantry Regiment, 4th Brigade Combat Team, 101st Airborne Division in Fort Campbell, Kentucky, died June 3, 2013, from wounds caused by a suicide bomber in Chamkani, Afghanistan.

NOTES:

Small

1000 meter Row

50 Burpees

50 Box jumps 24" box

800 meter Run

3 rounds for time

U.S. Army Staff Sergeant Marc Small, 29, of Collegeville, PA, assigned to 1st Battalion, 3rd Special Force Group (Airborne), based in Fort Bragg, NC, died on February 12, 2009, from wounds sustained when insurgents attacked his unit with a rocket-propelled grenade launcher and small arms fire in Faramuz, Afghanistan.

NOTES:

Smykowski

6 km Run

60 Burpee Pull-ups

For time
If you've got body armor or
a thirty pound vest, wear it.

U.S. Marine Corps Sergeant Mark T. Smykowski, 23, of Mentor, OH, assigned to 2nd Reconnaissance Battalion, 2nd Marine Division, II Marine Expeditionary Force, based in Camp Lejeune, NC, was killed on June 6, 2006, while conducting combat operations in Al Anbar province, Iraq.

NOTES:

Spehar

100 Thrusters
135lbs/61kg

100 Chest to Bar Pull-ups

6 miles Run

For time

U.S. Navy Special Warfare Operator Petty Officer 2nd Class (SEAL) Nicholas Spehar died Aug. 6, 2011, Wardak Province, Afghanistan, of wounds suffered when his helicopter was shot down. The 24-year-old, St. Paul, Minnesota, was assigned to a West Coast-based Naval Special Warfare unit and served during Operation Enduring Freedom.

NOTES:

Strange

600 meter Run

11 Weighted Pull-up
1.5 pood (apx 55lbs)

11 Steps Walking Lunge
carrying 1.5 pood Kettlebells

11 Thruster
1.5 pood Kettlebell

8 rounds for time

U.S. Navy Cryptologist Technician (Collection) Petty Officer 1st Class (Expeditionary Warfare Specialist) Michael J. Strange, 25, of Philadelphia, PA, assigned to an East Coast-based Naval Special Warfare unit, died on August 6, 2011, of wounds suffered when his unit's helicopter crashed in Wardak province, Afghanistan.

NOTES:

Stephen

Glute-Ham Sit-Ups

Back Extensions

Knees to Elbows

Stiff Legged Deadlift 95!

30-25-20-15-10-5 of all exercises

Third Battalion, Princess Patricia's Canadian Light Infantry member Corporal Stephen Bouzane, 26, was killed by an IED strike June 20th, 2007 in the Panjwaii district in Afghanistan.

NOTES:

Taylor

400 meter Run

5 Burpee Muscle-ups

4 rounds for time
If you've got a 20lb vest or
body armor, wear it.

U.S. Army Specialist David Wayne Taylor, 20, of Dixon, Kentucky, assigned to the 2nd Battalion, 508th Parachute Infantry Regiment, 4th Brigade Combat Team, 82nd Airborne Division, based in Fort Bragg, North Carolina, died in Kandahar province, Afghanistan on March 29, 2012, from wounds sustained in an accident at an ammunition supply point.

NOTES:

Terry

1 mile Run

100 Push-ups

100 meters Bear crawl

1 mile Run

100 meters Bear crawl

100 Push-ups

1 mile Run

For time

Drug Enforcement Administration Special Agent James "Terry" Watson, 43, of Holly Ridge, Louisiana, was killed during a robbery attempt in Bogotá, Colombia, on June 20, 2013. Prior to his 13 years of service with the D.E.A., Special Agent Watson worked for the U.S. Marshal's Service and served in the U.S. Army.

NOTES:

The Seven

7 Handstand Push-ups

7 Thruster 135lbs

7 Knees to elbows

7 Deadlift 245lbs

7 Burpees

7 Kettlebell Swings
2 pood (apx 72lbs)

7 Pull-ups

7 rounds for time

A suicide bomber killed seven CIA officers and one Jordanian officer at a remote base in southeastern Afghanistan on December 30, 2009 after posing as a potential informant reporting on Al Qaeda. Seven new stars will be etched onto the memorial wall at the CIA where every star represents grieving friends, family and colleagues dedicated to fight against the enemy, forever in their name. Killed in the attack were CIA officers Jennifer Lynne Matthews, 45; Scott Michael Roberson, 39; Harold E. Brown Jr., 37; Darren LaBonte, 35; Elizabeth Hanson, 30; and security contractors Jeremy Jason Wise, 35, and Dane Clark Paresi, 46.

Thompson

15ft Rope Climb 1 ascent

29 Back Squat
(M=95lbs, F=65lbs)

10 meter Barbells Farmer carry
(M=135lbs, F=95lbs)
10 rounds for time
Begin the rope climbs seated on the floor

U.S. Army Captain David J. Thompson, 39, of Hooker, OK, commander of Operational Detachment Alpha 3334, Company C, 3rd Battalion, 3rd Special Forces Group (Airborne), based in Fort Bragg, NC, was killed on January 29, 2010, while supporting combat operations in the Wardak Province of Afghanistan.

NOTES:

TK

8 Strict Pull-ups

8 Box Jumps 36" box

12 Kettlebell Swings
(M=2 pood/apx 72lbs, F=50lbs)

**As Many Rounds As Possible
in 20 minutes**

U.S. Army Major Thomas E. Kennedy, 35, of West Point, New York, assigned to Headquarters and Headquarters Company, 4th Brigade Combat Team, 4th Infantry Division, based in Fort Carson, Colorado, died on August 8, 2012, of wounds suffered when an insurgent detonated a suicide vest in Kunar province, Afghanistan.

NOTES:

Tom

7 Muscle-ups

11 Thruster 155lbs

14 Toes to Bar

As Many Rounds As Possible in 20 Minutes

U.S. Army First Lieutenant Thomas M. Martin, 27, of Ward, AR, assigned to the 1st Squadron, 40th Cavalry Regiment, 4th Brigade Combat Team (Airborne), 25th Infantry Division, based in Fort Richardson, AK, died on October 14, 2007 in Al Busayifi, Iraq, of wounds suffered when insurgents attacked his unit with small arms fire.

NOTES:

Tommy V

1. 21 Thrusters (M=115lbs. F=80lbs)

2. 15 Ft Rope Climb — 12 ascents

3. 15 Thrusters (M=115lbs. F=80lbs)

4. 15 Ft Rope Climb — 9 ascents

5. 9 Thrusters (M=115lbs. F=80lbs)

6. 15 Ft Rope Climb — 6 ascents

For time

In honor of Senior Chief Petty Officer Thomas J. Valentine, 37, of Ham Lake, Minnesota, died in an training accident in Arizona, on Feb. 13 2008.

NOTES:

Tully

200 meter Swim

23 Squat Cleans 40lbs Dumbbells

4 rounds for time

U.S. Army Sergeant First Class Michael J. Tully, 33, of Falls Creek, PA, assigned to the 2nd Battalion, 1s Special Forces Group (Airborne), based in Fort Lewis, WA, died on August 23, 2007, in Baghdad, Iraq, wounds sustained from an improvised explosive device.

NOTES:

Tumilson

200 meter Run

11 Burpee Deadlifts
60lb Dumbbells

8 rounds for time

U.S. Navy Special Warfare Operator Petty Officer 1st Class (SEAL/Enlisted Surface Warfare Specialist) Jon "JT" Thomas Tumilson, 35, of Rockford, IA, assigned to an East Coast-based Naval Special Warfare unit, died on August 6, 2011, in Wardak province, Afghanistan, of wounds suffered when his helicopter crashed.

NOTES:

T.U.P.

Power Cleans
135lbs/61kg

Pull-ups

Front squats
135lbs/61kg

Pull-ups

15-12-9-6-3 Reps for Time

U.S. Army Staff Sgt. Michael H. Simpson, of San Antonio, Texas, died May 1, 2013, in Landstuhl, Germany, from injuries caused by an improvised-explosive device on April 27, 2013, in Arian, Afghanistan. The 30-year-old, nicknamed "The Unquiet Professional," was assigned to the 4th Battalion, 1st Special Forces Group (Airborne), Joint Base Lewis-McChord, Washington.

NOTES:

Tyler

7 Muscle-ups

21 Sumo-Deadlift High-Pull
(M=95lbs, F=65lbs)

5 rounds for time

1LT Tyler E. Parten, 24, of Arkansas, died Sept. 10 in Konar province, Afghanistan, of wounds sustained when insurgents attacked his unit using rocket-propelled grenades and small arms fire. He was assigned to the 3rd Squadron, 61st Cavalry Regiment, 4th Brigade Combat Team, 4th Infantry Division, Fort Carson, CO.

NOTES:

Walsh

22 Burpee Pull-ups

22 Back squat
(M=185lbs, F=125/130lbs

200 meter Run with a 45lb plate overhead

4 rounds for time

U.S. Army First Lieutenant Jonathan P. Walsh, 28, of Cobb, Georgia, assigned to the 2nd Battalion, 504 Infantry, 1st Brigade Combat Team, 82nd Airborne Division, based in Fort Bragg, North Carolina, died o April 22, 2012, in Paktia, Afghanistan, when enemy forces attacked his unit with an improvised explosive device.

NOTES:

War Frank

25 Muscle-ups

100 Squats

35 Glute-Ham Sit-Ups

3 rounds for time

Captain Warren A. Frank, 26, of Cincinnati, Ohio, died November 25, 2008 while supporting combat operations in Ninewa province, Iraq. He was assigned to the 5th Air Naval Gunfire Liaision Company, III Marine Expeditionary Force, Okinawa, Japan.

NOTES:

Weaver

10 L Pull-ups

15 Push-ups

15 Chest to bar Pull-ups

15 Push-ups

20 Pull-ups

15 Push-ups

4 rounds for time

U.S. Army First Lieutenant Todd W. Weaver, 26, of Hampton, VA, assigned to the 1st Battalion, 320th Field Artillery Regiment, 2nd Brigade Combat Team, 101st Airborne Division (Air Assault), based out of Fort Campbell, KY, died on September 9, 2010, of wounds suffered when insurgents attacked his unit with a roadside bomb in Kandahar, Afghanistan.

NOTES:

Weston

1. 1000 meter Row

2. 200 meter Farmer carry 45lb Dumbbells

3. 50 meter Right arm Waiter Walk 45lbs Dumbbell

4. 50 meter Left arm Waiter Walk 45lbs Dumbbell

5 rounds for time

U.S. Drug Enforcement Administration Special Agent Michael E. Weston, 37, assigned to the Kabul Country Office in Kabul, Afghanistan, was killed on October 29, 2009, when the helicopter he was in crashed in western Afghanistan.

NOTES:

White

**15ft Rope Climb
3 ascents**

10 Toes to bar

21 Walking lunge steps with 45lb plate held overhead

400 meter Run

5 rounds for time

U.S. Army First Lieutenant Ashley White, 24, of Alliance, OH, assigned to the 230th Brigade Support Battalion, 30th Heavy Brigade Combat Team, North Carolina National Guard, based in Goldsboro, NC, died on October 22, 2011 in Kandahar province, Afghanistan, from wounds suffered when insurgents attacked her unit with an improvised explosive device.

NOTES:

Whitten

22 Kettlebell Swings
2 pood (apx 72lbs)

22 Box jump 24"

400 meter Run

22 Burpees

22 Wallballs

5 rounds for time

Army Captain Dan Whitten, 28, of Grimes, IA, assigned to the 1st Battalion, 508th Parachute Infantry Regiment, 4th Brigade Combat Team, 82nd Airborne Division, based out of Fort Bragg, NC, died February 2, 2010, when enemy forces in Zabul, Afghanistan attacked his vehicle with an improvised explosive device.

NOTES:

Willy

800 meter Run

5 Front Squat 225lbs

200 meter Run

11 Chest to Bar Pull-ups

400 meter Run

12 Kettlebell Swings (2 pood)

3 rounds for time

U.S. Marine Corps Sergeant Wade D. Wilson, 22, of Normangee, Texas, assigned to the 2nd Battalion, 5 Marine Regiment, 1st Marine Division, I Marine Expeditionary Force, based in Camp Pendleton, Californi died on May 11, 2012, while conducting combat operations in Helmand province, Afghanistan.

NOTES:

Wilmot

50 Squats

25 Ring dips

6 rounds for time

Wilmot, 24, of Fredericton, NB, assigned to the Second Battalion, Princess Patricia's Canadian Light Infantry (2 PPCLI) Battle Group, based out of Edmonton, AB, died on July 6, 2008 from wounds suffered when an explosive device detonated near him in the Panjwali District of Afghanistan.

NOTES:

Wittman

15 Kettlebell Swings
1.5 pood (apx 55lbs)

15 Power Clean
(M=95lbs, F=65lbs)

15 Box Jumps (M=24", F=18")

7 Rounds for time

U.S. Army Sergeant Jeremiah Wittman, 26, of Darby, MT, assigned to the 1st Battalion, 12th Infantry Regiment, 4th Brigade Combat Team, 4th Infantry Division, based out of Fort Carson, CO, was killed on February 13, 2010, when insurgents attacked his unit with a roadside bomb in Zhari province, Afghanistan.

NOTES:

Woehlke

4 Jerks
185lbs/83kg

5 Front Squats
185lbs/83kg

6 Power Cleans
185lbs/83kg

40 Pull-ups

50 Push-ups

60 Sit-ups

**3 rounds, each for time
Rest 3 min between rounds.**

Brian Woehlke, 29, of Detroit, Michigan, died at the scene of a fire in Westland, Michigan, on May 8, 2013. Woehlke graduated from the Schoolcraft Fire Program in 2008 and joined the Western Wayne Fire Authority in 2012.

NOTES:

Wood

1. 400 meter Run
2. 10 Burpee Box Jumps 24"

3. 10 Sumo-Deadlift High-pull (M=95lbs, F=65lbs)
4. 10 Thruster (M=95lbs, F=65lbs)

5 rounds for time
Rest 1 minute between each round

Australian Army Sergeant Brett Wood, 32, of Ferntree Gully, VIC, assigned to the 2nd Commando Regiment, based in Sydney, NSW, died on May 23, 2011, in Helmandprovince, Afghanistan, after insurgents attacked him with an improvised explosive device.

NOTES:

Zembiec

11 Back Squats, 185 lbs   **7 Strict Burpee Pull-ups***

400 meter Run

5 rounds for time

*During each burpee pull-up perform a strict push-up, jump to a bar
that is ideally 12 inches above your max standing reach,
and perform a strict pull-up.

U.S. Marine Corps Major Douglas A. Zembiec, 34, of Albuquerque, New Mexico, assigned to Headquarters Battalion, Marine Corps National Capital Region, Henderson Hall, based in Arlington, Virginia, was killed during a firefight on May 11, 2007 in Baghdad, Iraq.

NOTES:

Zeus

1. 30 Wallballs

2. 30 Sumo Deadlift High-pull
(M=75lbs, F=50/55lbs)

3. 30 Box Jumps, 20" Box

4. 30 Push Press
(M=75lbs, F=50/55lbs)

5. Row 30 calories

6. 30 Push-ups

7. 10 Back Squat Body Weight

3 rounds for time

U.S. Army Specialist David E. Hickman, 23, of Greensboro, NC, assigned to the 2nd Battalion, 325th Airborne Infantry Regiment, 2nd Brigade Combat Team, 82nd Airborne Division, based in Fort Bragg, NC died on November 14, 2011, in Baghdad, Iraq, from wounds suffered when insurgents detonated an improvised explosive device near his vehicle.

NOTES:

Zimmerman

11 Chest to Bar Pull-ups

2 Deadlifts 315lbs

10 Handstand Push-ups

As Many Rounds As Possible
in 25 minutes

U.S. Marine Corps First Lieutenant James R. Zimmerman, 25, of Aroostook, ME, assigned to 2rd Battalion, 6th Marine Regiment, 2nd Marine Division, II Marine Expeditionary Force, based in Camp Lejeune, NC, died on November 2, 2010, while conducting combat operations in Helmand province, Afghanistan.

NOTES:

The Open Workouts

11point1

30 Double Unders

15 Power Snatch
(M=75lbs/34kg F=55lbs/25kg)
As Many Rounds and Reps As Possible
in 10 minutes

NOTES:

11point2

9 Deadlifts
(M=155lbs/70kg F=100lbs/45kg)

12 Push-ups

15 Box Jumps
(M: 24" F: 20")

As Many Rounds and Reps As Possible
in 15 minutes

NOTES:

11point3

Squat Cleans
(M=165lbs/75kg F=110lbs/50kg)

Jerk
(M=165lbs/75kg F=110lbs/50kg)

5 min AMRAP

NOTES:

11point4

60 Bar-facing Burpees

30 Overhead squats
(M=120lbs/54kg F=90lbs/40kg)

10 Ring Muscle-ups

10 min AMRAP

NOTES:

11point5

5 Power Cleans
(M=145lbs/65kg F=100lbs/45kg)

10 Toes to bar

15 Wallballs
M: 20lbs/9kg to 10' target
F: 14lbs/6kg to 9' target

20 min AMRAP

NOTES:

11point6

Thrusters
(M=100lbs/45kg F=65lbs/29kg)

Chest to Bar Pull-ups

7 min AMRAP

Round 1: 3 Thrusters, 3 Chest to bar Pull-ups
Round 2: 6 Thrusters, 6 Chest to bar Pull-ups
Round 3: 9 Thrusters, 9 Chest to bar Pull-ups
Round 4: 12 Thrusters, 12 Chest to bar Pull-ups
Round 5: 15 Thrusters, 15 Chest to bar Pull-ups
Round 6: 18 Thrusters, 18 Chest to bar Pull-ups
Round 7: 21 Thrusters, 21 Chest to bar Pull-ups

This is a timed workout. If you complete the round of go on to 24. If you complete 24, go on to 27, etc.

NOTES:

12point1

Burpees
with a 6 inch touch

7 min AMRAP

Touch point must be 6 inches
above athletes max standing reach.

NOTES:

12point2

Snatch

Proceed through the sequence below completing as many reps as possible in 10 minutes of:

Round 1: Snatch, 30 reps (M=75lbs/34kg F=45lbs/20kg)
Round 2: Snatch, 30 reps (M=135lbs/61kg F=75lbs/34kg)
Round 3: Snatch, 30 reps (M=165lbs/74kg F=100lbs/45kg)
Round 4: Snatch, max reps in time remaining (M=210lbs/95kg F=120lbs/54

NOTES:

12point3

15 Box Jumps
(M: 24" F: 20")

12 Push Press
(M=115lbs/52kg F=75lbs/34kg)

9 Toes to bar

As Many Rounds and Reps As Possible
in 18 minutes

NOTES:

12point4

150 Wallballs
M: 20lbs/9kg to 10' target
F: 14lbs/6kg to 9' target

90 Double Unders

30 Muscle-ups

As Many Rounds and Reps As Possible
in 12 minutes

NOTES:

12point5
11point6 Redo

Thrusters
(M=100lbs/45kg F=65lbs/29kg)

Chest to Bar Pull-ups

7 min AMRAP
Note time once each round is completed.

Round 1: 3 Thrusters, 3 Chest to bar Pull-ups
Round 2: 6 Thrusters, 6 Chest to bar Pull-ups
Round 3: 9 Thrusters, 9 Chest to bar Pull-ups
Round 4: 12 Thrusters, 12 Chest to bar Pull-ups
Round 5: 15 Thrusters, 15 Chest to bar Pull-ups
Round 6: 18 Thrusters, 18 Chest to bar Pull-ups
Round 7: 21 Thrusters, 21 Chest to bar Pull-ups

This is a timed workout. If you complete the round of 21 go on to 24. If you complete 24, go on to 27, etc.

NOTES:

13point1

Burpees

Snatch

Proceed through the sequence below completing as many reps as possible in 17 minutes of:

Round 1: 40 Burpees, Snatch, 30 reps (M=75lbs/34kg F=45lbs/20kg)
Round 2: 30 Burpees, Snatch, 30 reps (M=135lbs/61kg F=75lbs/34kg)
Round 3: 20 Burpees, Snatch, 30 reps (M=165lbs/74kg F=100lbs/45kg)
Round 4: 10 Burpees, Snatch, max reps in time remaining (M=210lbs/95kg F=120lbs/54

NOTES:

13point2

5 Shoulder to overhead
M=115lbs/52kg F=75lbs/34kg

10 Deadlifts
M=115lbs/52kg F=75lbs/34kg

15 Box Jumps
(M: 24" F: 20")

As Many Rounds and Reps As Possible
in 10 minutes

NOTES:

13point3
12point4 Redo

150 Wallballs
M: 20lbs/9kg to 10' target
F: 14lbs/6kg to 9' target

90 Double Unders

30 Muscle-ups

As Many Rounds and Reps As Possible
in 12 minutes

NOTES:

13point4

Clean and Jerk
(M=135lbs/61kg F=95lbs/43kg)

Toes to bar

13 min AMRAP

Round 1: 3 Clean and Jerk, 3 Toes to bar
Round 2: 6 Clean and Jerk, 6 Toes to bar
Round 3: 9 Clean and Jerk, 9 Toes to bar
Round 4: 12 Clean and Jerk, 12 Toes to bar
Round 5: 15 Clean and Jerk, 15 Toes to bar
Round 6: 18 Clean and Jerk, 18 Toes to bar

This is a timed workout. If you complete the round of 18 go on to 21. If you complete 21, go on to 24, etc.

NOTES:

13point5

15 Thruster
(M=100lbs/45kg F=65lbs/29kg)

15 Chest to Bar Pull-ups

If 90 reps (3 rounds) are completed in under 4 minutes, time extends to 8 minutes.

If 180 reps (6 rounds) are completed in under 8 minutes, time extends to 12 minutes.

If 270 reps (9 rounds) are completed in under 12 minutes, time extends to 16 minutes, etc.

NOTES:

14point1
11point1 Redo

30 Double Unders

15 Power Snatch
(M=75lbs/34kg F=55lbs/25kg)
As Many Rounds and Reps As Possible
in 10 minutes

NOTES:

14point2

Overhead Squats
(M=95lbs/43kg F=65lbs/29kg)

Chest to Bar Pull-ups

Every 3 minutes for as long as possible complete

From 0:00-3:00
2 rounds of: 10 Overhead Squats, 10 Chest to Bar Pull-ups

From 3:00-6:00
2 rounds of: 12 Overhead Squats, 12 Chest to Bar Pull-ups

From 6:00-9:00
2 rounds of: 14 Overhead Squats, 14 Chest to Bar Pull-ups

etc., following same pattern until you fail to complete both rounds.

NOTES:

14point3

Deadlifts

15 Box Jumps
(M: 24" F: 20")

Complete as many reps as possible in 8 minutes of:

Round 1: 10 Deadlifts (M=135lbs/61kg F=95lbs/43kg), 15 Box Jumps
Round 2: 15 Deadlifts (M=185lbs/83kg F=135lbs/61kg), 15 Box Jumps
Round 3: 20 Deadlifts (M=225lbs/102kg F=155lbs/70kg), 15 Box Jumps
Round 4: 25 Deadlifts (M=275lbs/124kg F=185lbs/83kg), 15 Box Jumps
Round 5: 30 Deadlifts (M=315lbs/142kg F=205lbs/93kg), 15 Box Jumps
Round 6: 35 Deadlifts (M=365lbs/165kg F=225lbs/102kg), 15 Box Jumps

NOTES:

14point4

60 Calorie Rows

50 Toes to Bar

40 Wallballs
M: 20lbs/9kg to 10' target
F: 14lbs/6kg to 9' target

30 Cleans
(M=135lbs/61kg F=95lbs/43kg)

20 Muscle-ups

As Many Rounds and Reps As Possible
in 14 minutes

NOTES:

14point5

Thrusters
(M=95lbs/43kg F=65lbs/29kg)

Bar facing Burpees

21-18-15-12-9-6-3 Reps for Time

NOTES:

15point1

15 Toes to bar

9 Deadlifts
(M=115lbs/52kg F=75lbs/34kg)

15 Snatches
(M=115lbs/52kg F=75lbs/34kg)

As Many Rounds and Reps As Possible
in 9 minutes

NOTES:

15point1a

Clean and Jerk

1 Rep-max Clean and Jerk
6 min time cap

NOTES:

15point2
14point2 Redo

Overhead Squats
(M=95lbs/43kg F=65lbs/29kg)

Chest to Bar Pull-ups

Every 3 minutes for as long as possible complet

From 0:00-3:00
2 rounds of: 10 Overhead Squats, 10 Chest to Bar Pull-up

From 3:00-6:00
2 rounds of: 12 Overhead Squats, 12 Chest to Bar Pull-up

From 6:00-9:00
2 rounds of: 14 Overhead Squats, 14 Chest to Bar Pull-up

etc., following same pattern until you fail to complete bo
rounds.

NOTES:

15point3

7 Muscle-ups

50 Wallballs
M: 20lbs/9kg to 10' target
F: 14lbs/6kg to 9' target

100 Double Unders

As Many Rounds and Reps As Possible
in 14 minutes

NOTES:

15point4

Handstand Push-ups

Cleans
(M=185lbs/83kg F=125lbs/56kg)

8 min AMRAP following the rep scheme below:

Round 1: 3 Handstand Push-ups, 3 Cleans
Round 2: 6 Handstand Push-ups, 3 Cleans
Round 3: 9 Handstand Push-ups, 3 Cleans
Round 4: 12 Handstand Push-ups, 6 Cleans
Round 5: 15 Handstand Push-ups, 6 Cleans
Round 6: 18 Handstand Push-ups, 6 Cleans
Round 7: 21 Handstand Push-ups, 9 Cleans
Round 8: 24 Handstand Push-ups, 9 Cleans
Round 9: 27 Handstand Push-ups, 9 Cleans
Round 10: 30 Handstand Push-ups, 12 Cleans
Round 11: 33 Handstand Push-ups, 12 Cleans
Round 12: 36 Handstand Push-ups, 12 Cleans

etc., adding 3 reps to the handstand pushup each round, and 3 reps to the clean every 3 rounds.

NOTES:

15point5

Calorie Rows

Thrusters
(M=95lbs/43kg F=65lbs/29kg)

27-21-15-9 Reps for Time

NOTES:

16point1

25ft Overhead Walking Lunge
(M=95lbs/43kg F=65lbs/29kg)

8 Bar-facing Burpees

25ft Overhead Walking Lunge
(M=95lbs/43kg F=65lbs/29kg)

8 Chest to Bar Pull-ups

As Many Rounds and Reps As Possible
in 20 minutes

NOTES:

16point2

Toes to Bar

Double Unders

Squat Cleans

Beginning on a 4 minute clock, complete as many reps as possible of:
25 Toes to Bar, 50 Double Unders, 15 Squat Cleans (M=135lbs/61kg F=85lbs/38kg)

If completed before 4 minutes, add 4 minutes to the clock and proceed to:
25 Toes to Bar, 50 Double Unders, 13 Squat Cleans (M=185lbs/83kg F=115lbs/52kg)

If completed before 8 minutes, add 4 minutes to the clock and proceed to:
25 Toes to Bar, 50 Double Unders, 11 Squat Cleans (M=225lbs/102kg F=145lbs/65kg)

If completed before 12 minutes, add 4 minutes to the clock and proceed to:
25 Toes to Bar, 50 Double Unders, 9 Squat Cleans (M=275lbs/124kg F=175lbs/79kg)

If completed before 16 minutes, add 4 minutes to the clock and proceed to:
25 Toes to Bar, 50 Double Unders, 7 Squat Cleans (M=315lbs/142kg F=205lbs/93kg)

Stop at 20 minutes.

NOTES:

16point3

10 Power Snatches
(M=75lbs/34kg F=55lbs/25kg)

3 Bar Muscle-ups

As Many Rounds and Reps As Possible
in 4 minutes

NOTES:

16point4

55 Deadlifts
(M=225lbs/102kg F=155lbs/70kg)

55 Wallballs
M: 20lbs/9kg to 10' target
F: 14lbs/6kg to 9' target

55 Calorie Rows

55 Handstand Push-ups

As Many Rounds and Reps As Possible
in 13 minutes

NOTES:

16point5
14point5 Redo

Thrusters
(M=95lbs/43kg F=65lbs/29kg)

Bar facing Burpees

21-18-15-12-9-6-3 Reps for Time

NOTES:

The Nameless Workouts

For Time

1. 75 Push-ups
2. 50 Sumo-Deadlift High-Pull 95lbs
3. 50 Ring Dips
4. 30 Weighted Pull-ups 45lb
5. 25 Handstand Push-ups
6. 50 Ring Dips

For time

NOTES:

For Time

400 meter Run

50 Push-ups

400 meter Run

50 Handstand Push-ups

400 meter Run

For time

NOTES:

For Time

Handstand Push-ups

L-Pull-up

Round 1: 15 Handstand Push-ups, 1 L-Pull-up
Round 2: 13 Handstand Push-ups, 3 L-Pull-up
Round 3: 11 Handstand Push-ups, 5 L-Pull-up
Round 4: 9 Handstand Push-ups, 7 L-Pull-up
Round 5: 7 Handstand Push-ups, 9 L-Pull-up
Round 6: 5 Handstand Push-ups, 11 L-Pull-up
Round 7: 3 Handstand Push-ups, 13 L-Pull-up
Round 8: 1 Handstand Push-ups, 15 L-Pull-up

For Time

NOTES:

For Time

L-pull-ups

One legged squats, alternating legs

Round 1: 21 L-pull-ups, 20 One legged squats, alternating legs
Round 2: 18 L-pull-ups, 16 One legged squats, alternating legs
Round 3: 15 L-pull-ups, 12 One legged squats, alternating legs
Round 4: 12 L-pull-ups, 8 One legged squats, alternating legs

For Time

NOTES:

For Time

1. 21 L-Pull-up
2. 20 One legged squats, alternating legs
3. 18 L-Pull-up
4. 16 One legged squats, alternating legs
5. 15 L-Pull-up
6. 12 One legged squats, alternating legs
7. 12 L-Pull-up
8. 8 One legged squats, alternating legs

For time

NOTES:

For Time

Walking Lunge

Pull-ups

Sit-ups

Round 1: 100 ft Walking Lunge, 21 Pull-ups, 21 Sit-ups
Round 2: 100 ft Walking Lunge, 18 Pull-ups, 18 Sit-ups
Round 3: 100 ft Walking Lunge, 15 Pull-ups, 15 Sit-ups
Round 4: 100 ft Walking Lunge, 12 Pull-ups, 12 Sit-ups
Round 5: 100 ft Walking Lunge, 9 Pull-ups, 9 Sit-ups
Round 6: 100 ft Walking Lunge, 6 Pull-ups, 6 Sit-ups

For time

NOTES:

For Time

Hip-Back Extensions

Run

Round 1: 21 Hip-Back Extensions, 400 meter Run
Round 2: 18 Hip-Back Extensions, 400 meter Run
Round 3: 15 Hip-Back Extensions, 400 meter Run
Round 4: 12 Hip-Back Extensions, 400 meter Run
Round 5: 9 Hip-Back Extensions, 400 meter Run
Round 6: 6 Hip-Back Extensions, 400 meter Run
Round 7: 3 Hip-Back Extensions, 400 meter Run

For Time

NOTES:

For Time

Row

Push press 115lbs

Round 1: 400 meter Row, 21 Push press 115lbs
Round 2: 400 meter Row, 18 Push press 115lbs
Round 3: 400 meter Row, 15 Push press 115lbs
Round 4: 400 meter Row, 12 Push press 115lbs

For Time

NOTES:

For Time

Row

Burpees

Round 1: 1000 meter Row, 25 Burpees
Round 2: 750 meter Row, 50 Burpees
Round 3: 500 meter Row, 75 Burpees

For Time

NOTES:

For Time

GHD Sit-ups

Hip & Back Extensions

Thrusters 95lbs

Pull-ups

Round 1: 10 GHD Sit-ups, 10 Hip & Back Extensions, 30 Thrusters 95lbs, 50 Pull-ups
Round 2: 30 GHD Sit-ups, 30 Hip & Back Extensions, 20 Thrusters 95lbs, 35 Pull-ups
Round 3: 50 GHD Sit-ups, 50 Hip & Back Extensions, 10 Thrusters 95lbs, 20 Pull-ups

For time

NOTES:

For Time

Power Clean 155lbs

Ring Dips

Round 1: 15 Power Clean 155lbs, 30 Ring Dips
Round 2: 12 Power Clean 155lbs, 24 Ring Dips
Round 3: 9 Power Clean 155lbs, 18 Ring Dips
Round 4: 6 Power Clean 155lbs, 12 Ring Dips
Round 5: 3 Power Clean 155lbs, 6 Ring Dips

For Time

NOTES:

For Time

50 Box Jumps, 20" Box

15 ft Rope climb
5 ascents

50 Kettlebell Swing
1.5 pood (apx 55lbs)

50 Sit-ups

50 Hang Power Clean
40lb dumbbell

800 meter Run

50 Back extensions

For Time

NOTES:

For Time

5 Thruster 95lbs

10 Hang Power Cleans 135

10 Sumo-Deadlift High-Pull 95lbs

For Time

NOTES:

3 Rounds For Time

500 meter Row

21 Burpees

400 meter Run

3 Rounds For Time

NOTES:

3 Rounds For Time

12 Muscle-ups

75 Squats

3 Rounds For Time

NOTES:

3 Rounds For Time

6 Muscle-ups

30 Wallball 20lbs

12 Handstand Push-ups

15 Power Clean 135lbs

3 Rounds For Time

NOTES:

3 Rounds For Time

10 Deadlift 275lbs

50 Double unders

3 Rounds For Time

NOTES:

3 Rounds For Time

400 meter Run

30 Overhead squats 75lbs

21 Pull-ups

3 Rounds For Time

NOTES:

3 Rounds For Time

10 Weighted Pull-ups

30 Back Extensions

3 Rounds For Time

NOTES:

3 Rounds For Time

400 meter Run

15 Pull-ups

50 Squats

15 Pull-ups

3 Rounds For Time

NOTES:

5 Rounds For Time

1. 15 Hang Power Snatch 95lbs

2. 400 meter Run

5 Rounds For Time

NOTES:

5 Rounds For Time

400 meter Run

50 Squats

30 Back Extensions

5 Rounds For Time

NOTES:

5 Rounds For Time

3 Deadlifts

Handstand Push-ups, max reps

5 Rounds For Time

NOTES:

5 Rounds For Time

25 Kettlebell Swing
2 pood (apx 70lbs)

25 GHD Sit-ups

25 Back Extensions

25 Knees to Elbows

5 Rounds For Time

NOTES:

5 Rounds For Time

30 Glute-Ham Sit-ups

25 Back Extensions

5 Rounds For Time

NOTES:

5 Rounds For Time

20 Glute-Ham Sit-ups

5 Push jerk

5 Rounds For Time

NOTES:

5 Rounds For Time

10 Wall Climbs

10 Toes to Bar

20 Box Jumps, 24" Box

5 Rounds For Time

NOTES:

7 Rounds For Time

10 Sumo-Deadlift High-Pulls 95lbs

10 Ring Dips

7 Rounds For Time

NOTES:

7 Rounds For Time

3 Front Squat 185lbs

7 L-Pull-ups

7 Rounds For Time

NOTES:

As Many Rounds in 20 mins

250 meters Row

25 Push-ups

As Many Rounds As Possible in 20 minutes

NOTES:

As Many Rounds in 20 min

15 Clean & Jerk 95lbs

400 meter Run

As Many Rounds As Possible
in 20 minutes

NOTES:

As Many Rounds in 20 mins

10 Thrusters 65lbs

10 Pull-ups

As Many Rounds As Possible
in 20 minutes

NOTES:

As Many Rounds in 20 min

5 Handstand Push-ups

10 L Pull-ups

15 Steps, Walking Lunge

As Many Rounds As Possible
in 20 minutes

NOTES:

As Many Rounds in 20 mins

250 meter Row

21 Sumo-Deadlift High-Pull 95lbs

15 Pull-ups

As Many Rounds As Possible in 20 minutes

NOTES:

As Many Rounds in 20 min

15 Pull-ups

15 Ring Push-ups

15 Back Extensions

15 GHD Sit-ups

As Many Rounds As Possible
in 20 minutes

NOTES:

As Many Rounds in 20 mins

5 Chest to bar Pull-ups

10 Ring Dips

15 Overhead Squat 95lbs

As Many Rounds As Possible
in 20 minutes

NOTES:

Totals:

Full Clean:

Power Clean:

Back Squat:

Front Squat:

Full Snatch:

Power Snatch:

Split Jerk:

Clean & Jerk:

Deadlift:

Overhead Squat:

Press:

Push Press:

Push Jerk:

Conversion Chart

Weight (kg)	Weight (lbs)	Weight (kg)	Weight (lbs)	Weight (kg)	Weight (lbs)	Weight (kg)	Weight (lbs)
0	0.0	100	220.5	200	440.9	300	661.4
2.5	5.5	102.5	226.0	202.5	446.4	302.5	666.9
5	11.0	105	231.5	205	451.9	305	672.4
7.5	16.5	107.5	237.0	207.5	457.5	307.5	677.9
10	22.0	110	242.5	210	463.0	310	683.4
12.5	27.6	112.5	248.0	212.5	468.5	312.5	688.9
15	33.1	115	253.5	215	474.0	315	694.5
17.5	38.6	117.5	259.0	217.5	479.5	317.5	700.0
20	44.1	120	264.6	220	485.0	320	705.5
22.5	49.6	122.5	270.1	222.5	490.5	322.5	711.0
25	55.1	125	275.6	225	496.0	325	716.5
27.5	60.6	127.5	281.1	227.5	501.6	327.5	722.0
30	66.1	130	286.6	230	507.1	330	727.5
32.5	71.7	132.5	292.1	232.5	512.6	332.5	733.0
35	77.2	135	297.6	235	518.1	335	738.5
37.5	82.7	137.5	303.1	237.5	523.6	337.5	744.1
40	88.2	140	308.6	240	529.1	340	749.6
42.5	93.7	142.5	314.2	242.5	534.6	342.5	755.1
45	99.2	145	319.7	245	540.1	345	760.6
47.5	104.7	147.5	325.2	247.5	545.6	347.5	766.1
50	110.2	150	330.7	250	551.2	350	771.6
52.5	115.7	152.5	336.2	252.5	556.7	352.5	777.1
55	121.3	155	341.7	255	562.2	355	782.6
57.5	126.8	157.5	347.2	257.5	567.7	357.5	788.2
60	132.3	160	352.7	260	573.2	360	793.7
62.5	137.8	162.5	358.3	262.5	578.7	362.5	799.2
65	143.3	165	363.8	265	584.2	365	804.7
67.5	148.8	167.5	369.3	267.5	589.7	367.5	810.2
70	154.3	170	374.8	270	595.2	370	815.7
72.5	159.8	172.5	380.3	272.5	600.8	372.5	821.2
75	165.3	175	385.8	275	606.3	375	826.7
77.5	170.9	177.5	391.3	277.5	611.8	377.5	832.2
80	176.4	180	396.8	280	617.3	380	837.8
82.5	181.9	182.5	402.3	282.5	622.8	382.5	843.3
85	187.4	185	407.9	285	628.3	385	848.8
87.5	192.9	187.5	413.4	287.5	633.8	387.5	854.3
90	198.4	190	418.9	290	639.3	390	859.8
92.5	203.9	192.5	424.4	292.5	644.9	392.5	865.3
95	209.4	195	429.9	295	650.4	395	870.8
97.5	215.0	197.5	435.4	297.5	655.9	397.5	876.3
100	220.5	200	440.9	300	661.4	400	881.8

The official weights are in pounds. For your convenience, the minimum acceptable weights in kilograms are:
20 kg (45 lb.), 25 kg (55 lb.), 29 kg (65 lb.), 34 kg (75 lb.), 38 kg (85 lb.), 43 kg (95 lb.), 47 kg (105 lb.), 52 kg (115 lb.), 56 kg (125 lb.), 61 kg (135 lb.), 65 kg (145 lb.), 70 kg (155 lb.), 79 kg (175 lb.), 83 kg (185 lb.), 93 kg (205 lb.), 102 kg (225 lb.), 106 kg (235 lb.), 124 kg (275 lb.), 142 kg (315 lb.).
Wallballs: 9-kg ball (20 lb.), 6-kg ball (14 lb.), 4-kg ball (10 lb.).

CPSIA information can be obtained
at www.ICGtesting.com
Printed in the USA
BVOW11s1059010716
454100BV00003B/3/P